An Open Door

Papers from the Sanctuary and the Academy II

Bishop Earl G. Hunt, Jr.

An Open Door

Papers from the Sanctuary and the Academy II

Bishop Earl G. Hunt, Jr.

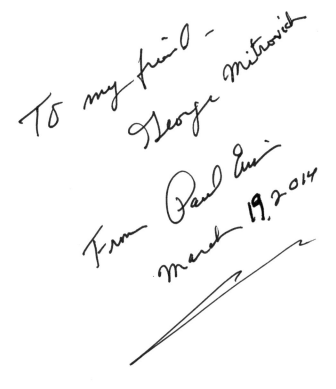

To my friend –
George Mitrovich

From Paul Ervin
March 19. 2014

First printing, October 2008

Printed in the United States of America

ISBN 10: 0-615-22835-6
ISBN 978-0-615-22835-6

Table of Contents

FOREWORD

For Bishop Earl Hunt the conjoining of learning and vital piety was not just a Wesleyan dictum but a way of life. His heart was in the Church and his passion was in evangelism, and like the Methodist founder, he not only preached, but read, wrote and studied all his life to the very end. In that he sought to emulate Wesley by being an example of how all of us should understand ministry and Episcopal leadership. This volume is testimony to that lifelong commitment and continues the conversation—even posthumously—regarding issues of vital concern to him and the Church.

All of us who knew him saw him as a towering figure, physically but also mentally and spiritually. Having come out of the academy, he knew how important the academy was for the integrity of the church, and how important the church was for the soul of the academy. Yet he never confused the two, and always respected the identity of each in its own sphere. But he also was convinced that they needed each other, and that an honest tension between them was necessary for their respective integrity. His wisdom in this area has over the years been crucial for us all and this volume is a welcome reminder of just how valuable his voice has been.

His great legacy was of course in evangelism. It is not often that the church has been blessed with one whose evangelistic heart was so enriched by a deep appreciation of church history and illumined by such immersion in scripture. This found enduring expression in the several chairs of evangelism that he was instrumental in establishing in our seminaries and his pivotal role in The Foundation for Evangelism. I count myself blessed in having worked with him to that end to establish the first chair at Candler. I also must take this opportunity to acknowledge my personal debt to Bishop Hunt. He was key to my coming to Emory as dean of Candler, serving as he did as the College of Bishops' representative on the search committee. As I was a virtual unknown at that time in the Southeast, he helped allay their understandable concern about the appropriateness of my appointment.

It was his judicious role in interpreting evangelism to a broader audience that gave it both appeal and a new currency in an era when many aspects of its expression had come under a cloud. Bishop Hunt was convinced, deep in his heart, that the joy and grace inherent in the gospel was good news to everyone, not the possession of some. He knew that only a church that was powered by such a motivation could grow. And he was determined to the end that such a spirit should animate the United Methodist Church. He was truly a bishop whose authority was the gospel and whose mantle was the robe of grace.

James T. Laney
President Emeritus, Emory University
Former U.S. Ambassador to South Korea

I

Offer Them Christ

I have loved every job my Church has ever given me. They have all been different. However, the total unexpectedness of coming into the presidency of The Foundation for Evangelism in 1989 brought me special joy and an unprecedented challenge, and caused me to become increasingly convinced that this particular opportunity was in quite an unusual way Providential.

There were gigantic problems the first year, and only the intercession of God Himself and the constant, vigorous support of an unswervingly loyal Board of Trustees made it all come out right.

My seven years in this office, and my nine subsequent years in an emeritus relationship, brought a literally magnificent valedictory blessing to my life.

(Dr. James C. Logan, a very close friend and the E. Stanley Jones Professor of Evangelism at Wesley Theological Seminary, was asked by Bishop Hunt to finish the last section of this chapter.)

Offer Them Christ

A Historical Overview

The title of this essay, taken from Kenneth Wyatt's epic painting, summarizes the mission of The Foundation for Evangelism. The Foundation itself was born in the fertile mind of Methodism's legendary lay executive Harry Denman in 1949. He organized it to be an adjunct of the General Board of Evangelism (later the General Board of Discipleship) and to create funding for evangelistic projects implemented by the General Board but not financed by it. The first three decades of The Foundation's history record a variety of such programs. The Foundation's list of trustees for this period reads like a Methodist Hall of Fame, containing the names of famous bishops and distinguished lay philanthropists—all of them distinctively evangelical and strong believers in Christian evangelism.

As the third decade of The Foundation for Evangelism drew to a close, its board of trustees began to discuss the employment of an executive director who was to be known as its president. After conversations with Dr. Charles E. Kinder of the Florida Conference, he accepted this position and came to work in The Foundation's Nashville offices (later moved to Lake Junaluska, North Carolina) in 1979.

The role of Charles and Phyllis Kinder in the life of The Foundation for Evangelism was memorable. His own account of it reminds one of the thrilling chapters of a best-selling novel. Dr. and Mrs. Kinder toiled relentlessly as they journeyed across this nation communicating the message of Christian evangelism to ordinary Methodist members and our denomination's elite leadership. The almost unbelievable active cooperation of celebrities like Tennessee Ernie Ford and Coach Tom Landry of the Dallas Cowboys was secured by the Kinders. Many of the present programs of The Foundation for Evangelism were instituted as the result of their genius. The most significant and far-reaching product of Dr. Kinder's creative mind may have been the establishment of evangelism as a legitimate discipline in the curriculum of the modern theological seminary. This had been attempted before the Kinder era, but its solid recognition came as Dr. Kinder and his board started professorships of evangelism at Boston University and Garrett-Evangelical Theological Seminary. The Kinders also discovered for The Foundation the eminent Christian artist Kenneth Wyatt who subsequently did the painting of John Wesley and Thomas Coke entitled "Offer Them Christ" (which became part of the logo of The Foundation), and later the paintings of Jesus and the Apostles. It should be noted that Dr. Kinder's extraordinarily able and generous Board Chairman, Mr. Robert E. Miller and his wife Joanie of Fort Smith, Arkansas, working with The Foundation's President, brought its capital worth to approximately one-million dollars. When Dr. Kinder resigned the presidency of The Foundation in 1989 because of ill health, he and his wife by their incredible devotion and indefatigable labors had left an organizational structure and a national image which were the strong base of The Foundation's future growth.

I was given the very high privilege of following Dr. Kinder as president of The Foundation for Evangelism for a period of seven years. An initial effort that we made was to celebrate the fortieth anniversary of The Foundation by the creation of an Evangelism Hall of Fame into which we inducted forty eminent church leaders, living and deceased, known for their evangelistic passion. The choosing of an additional member of this notable group each year thereafter became one of the most renowned programs sponsored by The Foundation. With the unusual abilities of my Board Chairman, Dr. John H. Marshall, Jr., one of this hemisphere's most noted geologists, and other remarkable members of our trustee family including David and Jean Stanley, Phillip Connolly, Mahlon McKinney, Bob Miller, and Roy Warren, we were able to establish additional professorships at St. Paul School of Theology, Wesley Theological Seminary, Duke University, Africa University and the Methodist Seminary in Reutlingen, Germany. We had two convocations on evangelism, one at Emory University featuring Christian leaders from around the world, and one at Wesley Theological Seminary featuring bishops of our church. The lectures given at these convocations were edited by Dr. James C. Logan and published in two anthologies by Kingswood Press, a division of Abingdon Press. The trustees increased the capital worth of The Foundation to something over five-million dollars. Dr. Curtis Schofield, former president of Hiwassee College, served for a period as Vice President for Development and assisted greatly in fundraising, inaugurating the Annual Conference Seventy (AC-70) program.

The most exciting and productive accomplishment in my seven years as president occurred in 1995 when the board of trustees employed a United Methodist attorney, Mr. Paul R. Ervin, Jr., to be Executive Vice President and Chief Operating Officer. Mr. Ervin, whose Christian dedication was almost beyond comprehension, at great but glad professional sacrifice, brought amazing gifts of organizational genius, in-depth knowledge of The United Methodist Church, fundraising skills, the best of legal minds and endless energy. Mr. and Mrs. Ervin, by their ceaseless travels, have created a widespread awareness of the existence and purpose of The Foundation for Evangelism among the leadership (particularly lay) of the church. The enormous increase in fiscal assets noted in the next two presidential administrations was largely the result of Paul Ervin's remarkable vision translated into ceaseless work.

As he put it to me one time, he does not have a job; he has a *calling*.

Bishop Ernest A. Fitzgerald served one memorable term as president of The Foundation, enlisting the vigorous assistance of new trustees including Mr. Royce Reynolds of Greensboro, North Carolina, and expanding the program agenda. Working in conjunction with the General Board of Discipleship, a churchwide program for small study groups entitled *Witness* was begun and splendidly received. Under the board chairmanship of Mr. Roy Warren of Englewood, Colorado, a prominent business executive deeply devoted to The Foundation and gifted in office operation, Bishop and Mrs. Fitzgerald were honored by the establishment of the Fitzgerald Institute Fund for evangelism and congregational development, and later by the launching of the Fitzgerald Program for New Church Pastors. During his administration, two more professorships were endowed and four were added increasing the number to eleven supported by The Foundation. The fiscal assets grew to nearly fifteen-million dollars.

In 2001 Bishop Richard C. Looney became president, bringing to The Foundation a distinguished image in the Council of Bishops and a lifelong commitment to Christian evangelism. In 2002 Mr. Lane Rees, Santa Rosa Beach, Florida, a veteran trustee with a profound and demonstrated interest in The Foundation, became chairperson of the Board of Trustees. Thus far, during the Looney presidency, and by Mr. Ervin's constant work and travels, a nearly unbelievable story of fiscal growth has been recorded resulting in the completion of the full endowment of nine professorships in the United States, two in Europe, one in Africa and one ecumenical professorship. Quite beyond this, operational endowment has grown significantly, the fund for a new headquarters building at Lake Junaluska has been completed, and an almost staggering amount of anonymous funding has been offered to underwrite essential new programs, including a doctoral program for professors of evangelism, a nationwide augmentation for youth and campus ministries and a greatly expanded use of the computer world through the Internet and websites.

I am convinced that one of the giant assets of The Foundation for Evangelism is its remarkably dedicated and gifted office staff, and I record here with my own profound appreciation the names of those who compose this select group: Bishop Richard C. Looney, President; Mr. Paul R. Ervin, Jr., Executive Vice President; Mrs. Lynda L. Leonard, Executive Assistant; Mr. William M. Hubbard, Business Manager; Mrs. Mary L. Burgin, Administrative Assistant; Mrs. Jane B. Wood, Project Manager; Mrs. Lynda L. Gibson, Bookkeeper; Mrs. Emily M. Hilfiker, Secretary; and James R. Crook, Resident Staff Minister.

As I write these lines, my memory recalls names like the late Mr. George Mathews, the late Dr. Ben D. St. Clair, the late Mrs. Conchita Blazer and Mrs. Mary Frances

Chappell, who transferred the assets of her late husband's evangelistic foundation to us and established the Wallace Chappell Lectureship on Evangelism for United Methodist seminaries in the United States. But over and above all of this is my own unmistakable conviction, and that of many others, that Almighty God has poured forth an unusual amount of Heaven's rich blessings upon The Foundation for Evangelism, placing upon all of us who have responsibility for this organization (or movement) an incredibly heavy obligation to be faithful to the stewardship that has been entrusted to us.

The Re-Appearance of Evangelism

Following the almost spectacular evangelical revival of the nineteenth century, there was a decided change (if not reaction) in the practical atmosphere of Christian America. In my own effort to understand what happened, I must record the fact that my analysis is that of a pastor and not what scholars and theologians might observe.

I was conscious, for one thing, of a theological factor in the fresh surfacing of the centuries-long attempt to discredit that doctrine of God known as *theism*. Again, I watched what occurred with the new science of Biblical criticism, which in its original intent was both constructive and helpful. Some Scriptural scholars, who seemed occasionally to lack their own experiential knowledge of the Christian faith, appeared to enter into what amounted to a gentle prostitution of the higher criticism study process in a way that dimmed confidence in the integrity of the Bible for many persons, including ministers and, consequently, made some of its basic doctrines less compelling. It was their viewpoints that gradually became the Biblical perspectives of denominational seminaries.

Furthermore, after the turn of the century the explanation of creation by the doctrine of *evolution* was accepted and espoused by the scientific and academic communities, raising fundamental questions about the teachings in the Book of Genesis. And coincidental with this was the widespread adoption of the scientific method as a basic formula for the thought process.

The result of these developments was the spread in many of the mainline churches of the Western world of a wave of religious liberalism which, while it had certain positive elements, virtually destroyed the fundamental passions of the evangelical viewpoint, making evangelism in many quarters an unclean word. This period of the prevalence of sweeping liberalism in the pulpits of this country and Europe lasted without serious challenge for nearly four decades.

Somewhere in the late 30s and the 40s another quiet change began to structure itself. Respected thinkers like Reinhold Neibuhr and John Bennett started an in-depth probing of the weaknesses of religious liberalism[1]. At about the same time and from an entirely different quarter, evangelical scholarship appeared in commanding fashion, and the pendulum started to swing. It was a slow process, particularly in many of the denominational seminaries. But the change seemed to take hold and to begin to spread once more across our nation, reaching the membership of the churches in far greater measure than their leadership. It was both ecumenical and international, and Dr. John Mackay, sometime president of Princeton Theological Seminary, referred to it as the "evangelical renaissance." Unquestionably the ministry of Billy Graham strengthened this movement. It has been constantly persistent and its amazing growth made it a factor in the 2004 presidential election in the United States. As one who was trained in a liberal seminary, I hasten to acknowledge that there are negative aspects attached at the moment to this development. The evangelical resurgence has not incorporated in its popular presence the strong evangelical scholarship which helped to form it. At the time of this writing much of it seems shallow. This has not helped the acceptability of the movement's evangelistic efforts. In fact, a few years ago true evangelism suffered a severe blow in the conspicuous appearance of a group of tele-evangelists whose basic motivation was monetary and not religious.

However, in spite of these negative factors, it can be said that the right kind of evangelism has achieved a strong positive image again in some of the mainline churches, particularly the United Methodist denomination. There is a sense in which this is a curious circumstance, for the "evangelical renaissance" has not yet been fully accepted by United Methodist leadership, specifically by some seminary faculty members and some members of the Council of Bishops. But the overwhelming truth is that a strong version of evangelism, the kind I shall attempt to describe in the next section of this paper, has now established itself as a primary part of the Christian mission in our church. Only this can explain from a human standpoint the phenomenal success of The Foundation for Evangelism in recent years. The re-appearance of evangelism is an authentic fact, and a glorious sign of hope!

Evangelism and The Christian Mission

Evangelism of the right kind, and properly understood, is the foundational thrust of the Christian mission in any evangelical church. The basic purpose of The Foundation for Evangelism has been to define evangelism in terms of its Biblical role and in keeping with the Wesleyan understanding of theology and practical churchmanship. This definition is informed by the "classical" meaning of Evangelicalism, but also by the solid and enduring emphases from the period of ecclesiastical liberalism. For the most part, the latter can be summed up in L. P. Jacks' memorable sentence, "The church is the union of those who love for the sake of those who suffer."

The principal problem true evangelism has had is that of establishing itself in a context of intellectual respectability where the academic community and the denominational leadership of the church are concerned. It is a fact that evangelism's simple proposal that a person should "accept Christ" must be made at some point in the evangelistic process, but oftentimes this has seemed to conclude the procedure, leaving the proposition without a supporting theology and with an obvious intellectual *thinness*. There are times when this is not only justifiable but also necessary, as when Jesus spoke to the thief on the cross, or when an effort is being made to win to God a dying individual. But this "thinness" has been used too frequently by thoughtful educated non-Christians and Christians to classify evangelism as inexcusably superficial.

It is absolutely essential for those of us committed to the restoration of evangelism as the primary part of Christian mission to achieve for it an image among questionable intellectual solidity. This is easily accomplished when the proper analysis is made. Evangelism's glorious simplicity is supported and validated by theological doctrines that compose in their fundamental richness the whole structure of Biblical Christianity.

We begin with the triune God of our holy faith. God the Father assumes the initiative in loving and seeking His children. God the Son (Jesus Christ) came to earth and died on the Cross to deal not only with all of human sin but also specifically with the sins of an individual person. God the Holy Spirit communicates to a man or a woman the entire message of Divine love and Divine forgiveness, and makes that person aware of the wonderful reality of salvation. The nature of the Heavenly Father, the sometimes complicated theology of the Cross and the ultimate fact of the Divine indwelling which comes to the child of God in what is sometimes referred to as being born again—these are all the magnificent Christian beliefs that constitute the structure of the evangelistic event.

Evangelism of the right kind should be both an event and a process. Sometimes the process will precede the event and at other times the event will need to come before the process. If there is a class of inquirers receiving instruction before the actual act of accepting the Christian faith, as is often true in a local church, then the process is preparation for the event. If, on the other hand, an invitation is extended in a series of spiritual life services or at the conclusion of a mass meeting or crusade, then the acceptance of the invitation is a prelude to whatever can be arranged as appropriate to follow-up instruction. In both instances, reference to meaningful Bible passages and the use of helpful literature should be features.

The evangelistic event, in either of the above situations, is properly only the beginning of a process of life-changing transformation which can go on for years. One other basic doctrine of the Christian faith has its place here. When an individual accepts Jesus Christ as Savior and Lord, that individual receives the Divine commitment that he or she will have life abundant here on this earth and life eternal in the world to come. In connection with the former, there is no promise that the human experience of the child of God will be free from the difficulties and the sorrows anyone experiences in his or her earthly pilgrimage. In the latter instance, we must acknowledge that one of the most precious of all Biblical promises, life beyond the grave, has suffered virtual eclipse in modern times. In thoughtful evangelical circles, a remarkable effort to restore the validity of this great doctrine seems now to be occurring[1].

The struggle to have evangelism accepted as an appropriate discipline in a seminary curriculum, for better or for worse, is a struggle to make it intellectually respectable. I have suggested that the recognition of its involvement with the great doctrines of the Bible is an appropriate and excellent way to achieve this. Another possibility lies with the baptismal vows and the vows of church membership, and once more it is to be assumed that in most instances some form of preliminary instruction will occur. The questions posed upon these occasions search the candidate's mental resources and involve the commitment of his or her will. The public acceptance of the obligations that attend the beginning of the Christian life go to the very roots of an individual's *raison d'etre* and involves anthropological as well as theological issues.

I believe that it is quite safe to say that The Foundation for Evangelism's efforts to establish the intellectual validity of the evangelistic task has already effected a substantial change in the way thoughtful Christians, particularly in the academic community, regard this whole matter. The high level of excellence achieved by our professors of evangelism in their classroom presentations and their intra-faculty relationships is responsible for this extremely hopeful development. Which is to say that in our own denomination and at some points elsewhere Christian evangelism is resuming its role in the Christian mission. This process will be accelerated and stabilized when the new doctoral programs for professors of evangelism are fully in place. It should also be noted that the books being written during this period by authors like James C. Logan and George Hunter are providing a brilliant literary support before the effort to elevate evangelism to the thought-level it occupied with John Wesley and Charles Grandison Finney.

Let me conclude this section of this essay by insisting that the right kind of evangelism will have its profound social results as well as its intimate personal meanings. When I was doing research for my graduate thesis on Dwight Lyman Moody, I came across a clipping from a Glasgow newspaper published a few years after the Moody-Sankey campaign in that Scottish city. It told of a great banquet held there to celebrate an anniversary of that evangelistic campaign. The eminent

British Bible scholar and friend of Mr. Moody, Sir George Adam Smith, was invited to deliver the principal address. When he arose to speak, he made no reference to evangelism but instead began to read a long list of social improvements that had come in the city of Glasgow during the last few years: prison reform, shorter hours, higher wages and better working conditions for laboring people, improved race relations, better care for the sick, the indigent and the orphaned, a finer quality of education, less drunkenness and a dramatically reduced crime rate. And he went on and on. Then he leaned over the lectern and said to his audience, "Every one of these improvements in this city is traceable, I can establish, to the visit here some years ago of two American lay evangelists and to the Gospel they preached that was based upon the Incarnation, the Atonement and the Resurrection of Jesus Christ, and the response that men and women made to that Gospel with their lives."

That is *real* evangelism at work not only in individuals but also in human society—and playing its role in the drama of the Christian mission!

Evangelism Within The Local Church[2]

Special programmatic emphases, preaching missions, and television spots have legitimate roles in a ministry of evangelism. What is absolutely essential to any faithful and effective ministry of evangelism, however, is a local congregation whose primary sense of identity is missional. In former times evangelism was compartmentalized with primary responsibility vested in the pastor and an evangelism committee. The American church in the twenty-first century finds itself in a new situation. Today the so-called mission field is at the very doors of the church. Some characterize our society as "neo-pagan," and others speak of the church in a "post-Christian" or "post-Christendom" time. Such a time calls for a re-conceiving of the local church's fundamental identity.

Bishop Lesslie Newbigin's *The Other Side of 1984: Questions for the Churches*, was a prophetic challenge to re-image the local congregation for a new day.[3] Newbigin's attempt to establish a new, and yet old, identity was to begin not with the church but with the very nature of God. Biblically, God is not a static being but a dynamic, outgoing God of grace. In biblical terms, God is a searching, finding, and sending God. Hence, God's people are those who have been found by the searching grace of God in Christ, and, hence, a faithful people of God will be those who mirror that outgoing nature of God in their individual and corporate existences. The fundamental identity of the church, therefore, is its concrete existence as a "sent" people.

Evangelism, reaching the unreached, is not the missional responsibility of a few select persons, but evangelistic outreach is, in one way or another, the responsibility of the whole congregation. For evangelism to be faithful and effective, what is essential is a congregational recognition that in their God-given DNA is an identity, not focused upon themselves, but upon the world which God in Christ has so loved. A faithful and effective evangelism ministry depends upon members of the local church sensing that being a missional people is not optional. Being a missional people is being faithfully who we are by the searching and finding grace of Christ. This does not mean that everyone is engaged in exactly the same actions of evangelism. Everyone, however, is engaged in one way or another in witnessing to the searching, finding, and sending God whom we see in the face of Jesus Christ.

What would such a local church or congregation look like if it were engaged in such a ministry of outreach and witness? Such a church would, first of all, be unapologetically Christ-centered. Civil religion has for decades pervaded our churches with a vague, generic theism. At best, God is viewed as a benevolent cosmic being. "God is love, and love is God." In truth, however, the God whom we see in Jesus Christ is the God of grace. Biblically speaking, grace is not some general divine benevolence. God is quite specifically the Source of "the grace of the Lord Jesus Christ." Grace is God's loving action in Jesus Christ embracing our lostness, brokenness, and, yes, sinfulness so that we may experience the forgiveness, reconciliation, and liberation which come only through Jesus Christ. By focusing unapologetically upon the forgiving grace of Christ and by experience that grace making us new creatures in Christ Jesus, we also discover that grace which is not shared is grace forfeited. Christ is both the source of evangelism and the object to which we witness.

What would a local church which takes its missional identity seriously look like? Such a church understands that the scriptural story is central and normative. We would not know anything about the person and work of Christ were it not for the scripture record. A missional congregation is found in and based on what the Bible teaches. This presents a real challenge for our day. Generally speaking, our local congregations manifest a biblical ignorance rarely if ever seen before in the history of the church. With all of the criticisms of the church, The United Methodist Church is doing one thing right! Hundreds of United Methodists are becoming biblically literate through Disciple Bible Study and other such programs. "The biblical witness is appropriated received as the testimony to God's mission and the formation of God's missionary people to be the instruments and witness of that mission."[4] As Augustine, Luther, Calvin and Wesley, among others knew in their bones, there is no renewal of the church without a recovery of the biblical message of salvation.

What would a local church which takes its missional identity seriously look like? Such a church would take the biblical message so seriously that its members would not be content simply to know "the story," but would be constantly pressing to put that "story" into action. As the epistle of James puts it, "Be doers of the word, and not merely hearers who deceive themselves" (James 1:27). A faithful evangelistic witness would take into account that salvation by grace means that we receive a divine *benefit*, the restoring grace of Christ, and simultaneously we receive a new *vocation*, a new calling. Defining evangelism as *benefit* without *calling* is a serious truncation of the biblical message. John Wesley certainly sensed this in his eighteenth century evangelical revival when he insisted upon the inseparability of *justification/sanctification.*

What would a truly missional church look like? A truly missional church is a people who practice biblical hospitality. This word has suffered in recent times. Today hospitality is simply another word for politeness. In the biblical world it is different. The story of Abraham and Sarai is illustrative. When the three strangers come down the road, Abraham invites them to sit with him. In other words, he makes space for the strangers. And when through Sarai's assistance the strangers are feted with a sumptuous meal, the tables are, so to speak, turned, and Abraham and Sarai hear the strange and exciting message, I will return in the spring, and Sarai shall have a child. A miracle is promised and in the spring the miracle is fulfilled. Making space for the stranger—that is biblical hospitality. For this reason, the epistle to the Hebrews makes the same point, "Be careful to practice hospitality to the stranger. Many have so done and found themselves entertaining angels unaware." A biblically missional church is one which constantly makes space for the stranger whoever that stranger may be.

If the local church is to experience a renewed sense of mission then these matters must be addressed with utter seriousness of intention. Then our preaching, teaching, institutional administration, and outreach in witness will take on new life in a new day.

II

The Right Kind of Evangelism

This brief essay appeared in the Circuit Rider for February 1997 and is used here with permission.

I re-read these paragraphs during the time this volume was under preparation and sensed the fact that my own philosophy of Christian evangelism has undergone refinement and a mild metamorphosis during the years of my Foundation for Evangelism presidency. Some of its new maturity may be in evidence in this piece of writing. It is also significant that I elected to begin my article with a reference to D. L. Moody in Gamaliel Bradford's famous psychograph.

My review of this article did not reveal to me any point that I would elect to change.

The Right Kind of Evangelism[1]

"....God is the one supreme universal need of all humanity.... If he does exist, life should be but one long effort to know him and be at one with him.... The power of molding souls is the greatest power in the world...." These three sentences, written seventy years ago, are from the pen of the great American biographer Gamaliel Bradford, himself a gentle agnostic, in his brilliant psychograph entitled *D. L. Moody: Worker in Souls*.[2] To me they still suggest the classical reasons why the task of the evangelist has always demanded unassailable priority in the life of the Christian church from the far away days of Chrysostom and John Donne to the modern era of Billy Graham.

There have been, of course, periods in Christian history when this priority has seemed to be in eclipse, one such in recent decades. This has been so particularly in the theological arena which ultimately exerts substantial influence on local church pastors. Professor William J. Abraham, who holds the Albert C. Outler Chair at Perkins School of Theology, has examined this problem at length in his book *The Logic of Evangelism*.[3] Among other factors, he mentions the assumption by the churches of Europe and America (where Christianity has in the past been so strong) that evangelism is no longer necessary. He points out also that academic theology has been consumed by other concerns and has often felt that the "minor motif" of evangelism demands "prior faith commitments" that corrupt the capacity for critical evaluation of other issues. I appreciate Dr. Abraham's observations. However, my experience as an officer of The Foundation for Evangelism in working with our church's seminaries has given me reason to hope that the scene is shifting and that the circumstances he poses are being altered presently (especially among the administrators of our theological institutions).

A Struggle to Achieve Identity

Christian evangelism is struggling to achieve a positive contemporary identity. A growing segment of our church leadership seems to be realizing that evangelism is an authentic, desperately needed, often sorely neglected aspect of United Methodism's total mission. It is true that a smaller group, occasionally quite vocal, continues to resist any evangelism renaissance for reasons that deserve attention. One of these is the negative image acquired for evangelism by some of its unfortunate proponents. Another is what some regard as the ethical problem of proselytization in an era of religious pluralism. A third is the loss in some quarters of the traditional belief in the uniqueness of Jesus Christ. More clearly discernible is a much larger company of United Methodists, leaders and members, who appear to be innocently apathetic about the entire issue.

But the struggle goes on. Let me mention here two hopeful signs that a new concern for the right kind of evangelism may be developing. The first is the overwhelming action of the 1996 General Conference in declaring simply and unequivocally that "The mission of the [United Methodist] church is to make disciples of Jesus Christ." This in itself is *quintessential* evangelism! The second sign is the manner in which United Methodist seminaries increasingly are accepting the fact that evangelism is or can be a valid discipline to be offered in their academic curricula. At least eleven of our institutions in this country, and two in other parts of the world, presently have, or plan to have in the immediate future, professorships of evangelism.

Complicating Factors

As this century closes, effective evangelism must do its work in a world profoundly influenced by a cluster of complicating factors, including the following:

1. The Information Age with its nearly incredible digital technology, all of which has unavoidable implications for religious communication.
2. An accelerated critical evaluation of the Biblical record.
3. Rapidly changing cultural mores.
4. Religious pluralism, with a highly visible growth in our country of Islamic, Buddhist and other non-Christian faiths. Dr. Abraham's intriguing idea of the "Cosmic Christ" at work in other religions may be helpful here, even if it should prove to be unacceptable to some evangelicals.
5. A widespread impact from religious syncretism and theological universalism.
6. A highly secularized society directly and indirectly influenced by the kind of humanistic thinking from which the ideas of the supernatural and the eternal are radically absent.
7. An ecclesiastical *milieu* in which the concept of expansion is dominated by the sometimes theologically inadequate philosophy of the church growth movement and the flourishing phenomenon of the megachurch.

Recent books by Dr. George G. Hunter III[4] and other authors have lodged the idea of the megachurch deeply in our thinking, and even those of us who have held different perspectives must acknowledge the remarkable growth of these contemporary, often non-traditional congregations, together with the fact that they are reaching multiplied thousands of un-churched, "pre-Christian" persons, as well as many others. We can salute them, and still raise serious questions that have to do with their theological and Biblical depth, their proper emphasis on social aspects of the gospel, their knowledge of Christian history and doctrinal integrity, and the apparent absence of the kind of "connectedness" that is able to impact strongly both community and national life.

Propositions for Dialogue

I venture to suggest certain propositions which I believe to be worthy of serious consideration and dialogue as United Methodist clergy and laity strive to help evangelism become a greater force in the life of our church than it has been in recent years.

1. The *leadership* of the church must come to believe again in the *urgent priority* of evangelism. Presently it does not, or at least its words and actions do not indicate that it does.

2. The *message* of evangelism must be deeply rooted in the central truths of the Bible and Wesleyan theology, and must seek to express these truths in understandable language for new generations. The message always must be that of an evangelism both *personal* and *social*.

3. The *motivation* for evangelism must reside in a deep desire to bring persons into a redemptive, living relationship with God through Jesus Christ, and must remain separated from statistical goals and the idea of mere institutional prosperity.

4. The *design* of evangelism must reflect a sensitive knowledge of this complex post-Christian, post-modern era of human history.

5. The *focus* of evangelism must be not only upon the *soul* of a person but also upon an individual's *mind* and *will*. Both prejudices and commitments need to be redeemed.

6. The *scope* of evangelism must be *totally inclusive*, reaching persons of all races, creeds, cultures, economic and educational levels, sexual persuasions and moral conditions.

7. The *end* of evangelism is transformation, changed lives. *Valid evangelism should always eventuate in discipling*, but it is forever the Holy Spirit's work, and the achievement is God's achievement. Our task is to provide the witness. I once saw a sign over a church door in New England which said, "Broken lives repaired here." Our church choir sang recently the African-American spiritual "Fix Me, Jesus!" The two clauses in quotation marks suggest to me both the purpose and the possibility of true evangelism, as well as the foundational work of our church in any generation.

I deeply believe that the sentences from Bradford's psychological study of Mr. Moody with which I began this article actually constitute an unintentional but thoughtful human commentary on the many Scriptural passages that mandate the practice of evangelism. In spite of the fact that my own ministry of more than half a century for the most part has been identified proudly with Christian higher education, I am convinced that nothing is more important at this moment in the life of United Methodism than *the right kind of evangelism*. My confident hope is that our church will turn increasingly in this direction as the new millennium approaches, and that this trend will include and involve both sincere liberals and sincere conservatives.

Endnotes

[1]   This essay appeared in the *Pulpit Digest*, February 1997. Used by permission.

[2]   Gamaliel Bradford, *D. L. Moody: A Worker in Souls.* Garden City, NY: Doubleday, Doran & Co., Inc., 1928.

[3]   William J. Abraham, *The Logic of Evangelism.* Grand Rapids, Michigan: William B. Eerdmans Publishing Co., 1989.

[4]   George G. Hunter III, *How To Reach Secular People.* Nashville, Abingdon Press, 1992. *Church For The Unchurched.* Nashville, Abingdon Press, 1996.

III

An Open Door

This was the Ordination and Consecration Sermon which I preached at Calvary United Methodist Church, Nashville, Tennessee, in June 1986.

I deeply appreciated the hospitality of Bishop and Mrs. Ernest W. Newman, who were valued members of my cabinet family in Florida before his election to the episcopacy. I love them both and often re-live in my mind memories associated with them. Mrs. Newman, in my judgment, is the unofficial national winner of any contest involving baseball scores and batting averages! Bishop Newman is a statesman of the church.

This was a splendid opportunity for me to be back among my many, many friends in the historic Tennessee Conference, a place which is rich in the annals of our church and the Volunteer State. Mary Ann and I loved our four years there and were saddened because circumstances did not permit us to remain another quadrennium. Some of the very great personalities we have known in our episcopal career are prominent members of the Tennessee Conference. Another memory which keeps flashing itself before my mind is the wonderful Vanderbilt University Dining Club which I frequented quite often and where, among others, I visited with Dr. Harvie Branscomb, Chancellor Emeritus of the University and the author of the text we used in my classes in New Testament at Candler School of Theology, Emory University.

An Open Door

Bishop Newman, my dear Christian friends:

Let me say that the honor of being invited by your bishop to be part of this Annual Conference and to have the privilege of this particular message is a pleasure I shall long cherish. Mary Ann and I have left a deposit of service here, but we have carried away a treasure of memories greater than any deposit of service. The Tennessee Annual Conference will always have for us a special place of deep affection and gratitude in our hearts and lives. To be with your bishop and his dear wife, two of the loveliest Christian people we have ever known and two of the finest members of a cabinet family I have ever had, is an added joy and a very distinct honor.

I read to you a verse of Scripture first from the Revised Standard Version and then from the New English Bible, Colossians 4:3: "And pray for us also that God may open for us a door for the word to declare the mystery of Christ." And then in the New English Bible, again this great Pauline utterance: "Include a prayer for us that God may give us an opening for preaching to tell the secret of Christ."

I have five simple words for us tonight—*awareness, vision, preaching, practicum* and *epiphany*.

First, *awareness*. It was Mr. Justice Holmes who said it is required of a person that he shall share the passion and action of his time on penalty of being judged not to have lived. Which is to say that unless you and I are able to focus upon *our own moments* in human history, we miss the entire target. Our moment has its own plethora of specific problems. The few I name are but suggestive of others: the continuing inroads of the moral and sexual revolutions, the changing concepts of education, the problems of sexism, ageism and racism, a vast economic revolution with struggles to protect American products from foreign imports and to confront and control the menace of hostile mergers at home, the nuclear threat now lodged principally in the irresponsibleness of small nations, environmental perils, the expansion of our Southland from a two or three race region to one representing the full ethnic minorities spectrum, the fear of terrorism throughout our world, famine, AIDS, Alzheimer's disease, cancer, et cetera, et cetera. One could go on and on interminably. But these are only the specific detailing of three larger, overarching problems.

The first of these is the problem of *self-aggrandizement*, selfishness, a human being playing God, the whole tragic scenario that began in the Garden of Eden. The second is the *struggle between despair and hope*. The little girl prayed her childish prayer for all of us: "And, God, take good care of yourself, 'cause if anything happens to you, we're all sunk." And the third is *the failure of will*. Years ago Alexander Solzhenitsyn's classic address prepared for the occasion when he was to receive his Nobel award, referred to the principle problem of our time as being the resurgence of the spirit of Munich[1], the collapse of the human will. Be assured of this, dear Christian friends who are to be consecrated and ordained this evening, this is a different moment from any moment in all of the annals of the centuries. Thus, the first word I have for you and for myself is *awareness*.

The second word is *vision*. I think, as I hope you do, first of all, of the importance of the local church, the local parish, which is always where the action is and is that for which all of the other structures of a vast denomination like ours exist. Your contribution to the pulpit, to the ministry of visitation, to the building of the Sunday School and the whole educational task of the local church will be pivotal in the determination of the influence and the efficacy of that church in the days and years that lie ahead. And yet there is so much more than the local church. We are still under the Great Commission, "Go ye therefore and teach all nations, baptizing them in the name of the Father and of the Son and of the Holy Spirit." A Christian minister, or a Christian layperson, is compelled to acquire a worldwide vision in order that he or she may see far, far beyond what is *immediate*. Somebody asked William Blake one time, "When you look at the sun do you not see a bright disk about the size of a half crown?" William Blake laughed and said, "No, when I look at the sun I see a multitude of the heavenly hosts, praising God and singing to His glory." Somehow we have to break out of the confines of our little, narrow, parochial perspective upon life. There is a world out there, a world for which the Son of God died. Karl Barth used to write about the incurable God-sickness of a human being, and Arthur Compton, that great Nobel laureate who was a member of our own denomination, reminded us that science has created a world in which Christianity becomes an imperative. The lens through which the Christian beholds life is always *bi-focal*. We see that which is near at hand, the local church with its inevitable challenge, but we see also that which is farther away, the world for which Christ gave himself.

> "I know of lands that are sunk in shame
> Of hearts that faint and tire,
> But I know a Name, a Name, a Name
> That can set those lands on fire."

Thus, I leave with you my second word, *vision*.

The third word that I speak is *preaching*. The great city of Northern Germany is Hamburg, the home of our daughter-in-law, and on our visits there my wife and I have been driven by St. Michael's Church, where is located one of the most influential pulpits in all of Europe. It was from this pulpit some years ago that Professor Helmut Thielicke, the continent's prince of preachers, proclaimed with power the Christian gospel. In one of his books he wrote this provocative sentence: "Anybody who knows the goals of the Reformation can only be appalled at what has happened to the church of Luther and Calvin (and he might have added Wesley) whose leaders were convinced that a certain thing was the spring and source of faith and life, and that thing," said Dr. Thielicke, "is preaching."

Down in Florida we had an epidemic of *ten-minute* sermons. We also had an epidemic of carefully and esthetically constructed liturgical services that deliberately and obviously placed the sermon in a position of secondary or tertiary importance in the whole experience of worship. I suggest to you that neither of these will bring about a renaissance of the Christian faith in your time or mine. I further suggest to you that either is a prostitution of the Protestant and the Wesleyan viewpoint about worship. Preaching is at the center, the proclamation of the Word of God, the sharing of the mystery of Christ. This was what Paul was pleading that they should pray for him to have, an opening of a place to do this, *to preach*.

The preacher, I think, should always have five qualities. *First*, he or she should have a *personal knowledge of the living God and his gospel*, should know God, as Carlyle said, other than by hearsay. *Second*, the preacher should *work hard*. Many of the problems of the contemporary parish could be obliterated by intentionally industrious preachers. *Third*, there should be a *nearly frightening sense of urgency*. When I go to church even in my own denomination, the denomination of Wesley, I sometimes hear lovely little essays given in the place of sermons. Last night when I went back to my hotel from Conference, I listened to a breathtaking performance by Leonard Bernstein, directing the Vienna Philharmonic Orchestra in some of the works of Strauss. I watched Leonard Bernstein as he lost himself in the agony and ecstasy of making music. I watched him as he swayed back and forth at the podium and as his beautiful evening attire became visibly disheveled because of the energy, physical and emotional, which he poured into that performance. I found myself wishing that men and women who proclaim the gospel would become as deeply moved about that as Bernstein was about Strauss.

Fourth, a preacher must *love human beings*, not en masse but as individuals. The Pilgrims used to pray a prayer, "Give me the gift of tears." Oh, how we need again the gift of tears, until it really matters to us whether or not a man or a woman knows God!

Then, *fifth*, there must be *believing prayer*. A sermon is different from a classroom lecture, different from a travelogue, different from a news commentary. Only saturation in prayer will open the gates of Heaven for the blessing of God to work through that sermonic offering. Many times, as I have preached, I have silently prayed that my often inadequate words would be taken up by the Spirit of God and given wings to carry them into the hearts of my hearers, and I have watched as this literally happened and God used a very ordinary bit of preaching to bring to pass extraordinary results.

Therefore, the third word (and a very important word it is) is *preaching*.

The fourth word is *practicum*. To be sure, I recommend obedience to the Ten Commandments, but I give you tonight ten minor commandments. *One*, keep your marriage strong, grow together. It will be the best sermon you ever preach. *Two*, handle your jealousies or they will handle you, and they will make you sick and destroy your ministry. *Three*, attend district and Conference meetings, for you and I have been given the stewardship of a thing called *connectionalism*, and it requires constant and careful nurture. *Four*, master your grammar. Don't ever allow the grandeur of your insights about God to be obliterated by your ignorance of the proper case to follow a preposition. *Five*, avoid scandal. There are some problems a preacher does not need to have, if he or she is willing to take the proper precautions. *Six*, deal with your own temptations. When I was young, I once faced a temptation to speak with unnecessary cruelty about a fellow human being. A part of me that knew this was terribly wrong looked up to God, and suddenly a Heavenly Presence seemed to stand by me. My temptation left and my self-respect remained intact. Deal with your temptations.

Seven, respect the laity and learn from them, particularly from those with whom you disagree. *Eight*, keep clean and attractive. Always present your best appearance, and of all the cosmetics you purchase, be sure that one forever with you is a container of deodorant. *Nine*, never tell dirty jokes and never use questionable language, for such will tarnish your gospel. *Ten*, pay your debts and if you cannot pay them now, make satisfactory arrangements to pay them as soon as possible. If I had another commandment to give you just for good measure, it would be, *watch your health*.

Last of all, *epiphany*. We have to keep the epiphanies happening in our lives. We have to keep our eyes upon the mountaintops, even while we plod through the valleys. You are going to have trouble keeping your dreams fresh, and dreams are the fuel of the soul. There will be many times when you will have to reach down and pick them up, broken and shattered around your feet, and dust them off and put them together again, for you cannot live, you cannot preach, you cannot minister without dreams. Do you remember Jeremiah 29:11: "I know the dreams that I have dreamed of you, saith the Lord, dreams of peace and not of war, to give you an afterward and the things that you long for." [2]

A genuine experience of epiphany requires that the emphasis shall remain always upon the Lord, and that the recipient of this blessing shall be humbly grateful that this touch of Heaven's power has come to him or to her.

Wonder of wonders, "unto me who am less than the least of all the saints is this grace given, that I should preach among the Gentiles the unsearchable riches of God" (Ephesians 3:8). This is gratitude bathed in awe on the part of St. Paul— gratitude especially for the manner in which Jesus Christ has transformed life and replaced its weakness with his power. How many of God's own children have there been in my own years who have helped the Master accomplish this in me!

One of them has a son-in-law who is a distinguished member of this Annual Conference. I was seated in my office in Lakeland, Florida a few years ago, and my secretaries had been told that they must not interrupt me for any reason because I was preparing an address that had to be given soon. I was closeted with my books and my thoughts. All of a sudden I heard a voice. It was low at first and genteel, and then I heard the murmuring protests of two greatly dedicated and thoroughly instructed secretaries. Then that first voice began to rise until it took on stentorian qualities. I stopped what I was doing and listened through the wall and the door until I recognized the voice, and this is what I heard: "You say I can't see him; I helped bring him up! You tell Earl I've come." I knew he'd come, there was every evidence of that, and I threw open the door. I saw these terribly frustrated, wholly intimidated secretaries standing there nonplused, utterly helpless. I opened my arms wide and George Atkinson raced to me and we embraced each other. In a little while he brought his wife in and I called Mary Ann and we sat down and had a magnificent visit reconstructing memories that had helped us become not only the children of God, but also the ministers of Christ. Be grateful. Never forget such friends, and remember, in this struggle to keep epiphanies in your life, the words of Pierre Teilhard deChardin, "Jesus Christ is the Omega point, the destination to which all roads of truth lead at last." Hear Paul: "And pray for us also that God may open to us a door for the word to declare the mystery of Christ."

All that I have tried to say on this magnificent occasion for those who are to be consecrated and ordained can be gathered up in a brief paragraph from the man many regard as the greatest preacher in the English language in the last half of the twentieth century, Professor James S. Stewart of the University of Edinburgh: "Bring everything you have and are to the ministry—bring it without reserve— but when you have brought it, something else remains: Stand back and see the salvation of God!"

Endnotes

[1]   Neville Chamberlain's disastrous compromise with Adolph Hitler which became the prologue to World War II.

[2]   This is a free translation used by Mrs. Grace Livingston Hill, famous American Christian novelist, in an address to young people.

IV

In The Country of The Young

This sermon was delivered in the morning of October 18, 1970 at the Chapel of Duke University in Durham, North Carolina, upon the occasion of the inauguration of former Governor Terry Sanford as President of the University. There is a sense in which this paper is a period piece, dealing as it does with that memorable era of the sixties and early seventies when campus rebellion was the order of the day across our country.

My carefully constructed, perhaps nearly verbose, description of a typical student, more likely male, derives from my own exposure to campus life as a college president prior to my election to the episcopacy.

I wish I could pay an adequate tribute to Terry Sanford, whose distinguished tenure at Duke was followed by a period as United States Senator from North Carolina, and especially as a thoughtful, gifted layperson of United Methodism. I had many associations with him while I was bishop of the Charlotte Area, and others while I was in Florida. He was a churchman par excellence and an utterly delightful human being.

This address was published in the Duke Alumni Register, and is used with permission.

In The Country of The Young

Text: Ezekiel 3:15 *"Then I came to them of the captivity at Tel-a-bib, that dwelt by the river of Che-bar, and I sat where they sat, and remained there astonished among them seven days."*

President and Mrs. Sanford, dear friends:

The life of the university and the auspicious occasion which marks the inauguration of its distinguished new president are inextricably interwoven with the theme of youth. This is that with which they have to do—or there is neither rhyme nor reason for this place or this day. So, in a context of deep appreciation for this important institution, joined so very intimately to the church by its basic documents, and in vigorous hope for the administration of President Sanford, I am honored to present on his special day my theme "In the Country of the Young"—a title borrowed from Professor John Aldridge's essay in *Harper's* last October.

I have taken as a text a very familiar sentence from Ezekiel, chapter 3, verse 15: "Then I came to them of the captivity at Tel-a-bib, that dwelt by the river of Che-bar, and I sat where they sat, and remained there astonished among them seven days."

The setting is an interesting one. Ezekiel, following his vision of the glory of Yahweh and his commission to undertake the task of a prophet of God, had in all probability repaired in the fifth year of the exile of King Jehoiakin to his own hometown in Babylonia, a place called Tel-a-bib built on a low mound created by the flood, whose name meant "hill of young ears" (of barley). There he had a house and there he could maintain his association with the exiles dwelling by the river Che-bar. Ezekiel's problem was to reconcile his glimpse of glory with the nitty-gritty facts of his moment in history. He had been given a task but not told how to accomplish it. He understood the idealism of his new knowledge but not its implementation. The vision had passed but its power lingered—only now he was baffled by what might be involved in causing the vision to live in that part of society for which he had been given responsibility. But he had basic good judgment: he knew he could not ignore his fellows and he could not work out his mission in isolation from them and their influence. Therefore, he spent a memorable week in their midst, listening to them, talking with them, evaluating their viewpoints, as he struggled to understand what God wished him to do. He "sat where they sat."

What a picture of today! What a picture of the church undertaking to structure the kind of society of which youth at its best dreams! What a picture of higher education endeavoring to apply its vision of knowledge and its meaning to a new day, a new generation, a new earth! What marching orders for all of us who live "in the country of the young!" The serious alienation which we ordinarily refer to as the generation gap confronts the Christian community at once with its most serious task and its most exciting opportunity. Surely one of the critical missions of the church and the church-related university at this moment is to discover effective ways to bridge that gap.

Let me attempt to suggest four approaches.

We Must Listen and Understand

I am convinced that this is the first step to be taken. A distinguished American educator said in a recent address that one problem of which contemporary youth are painfully aware is the plain fact that they are not getting a respectful hearing from their elders. One is reminded of the late Adlai Stevenson writing in his book *A Call to Greatness*, "I sometimes think what Americans need more than anything else is a hearing aid!" In seeking material for this message, I had occasion to examine a great many relevant volumes representing reasonably recent additions to my own library, discovering to my dismay that in 32 of these neither tables of contents nor indices made any reference whatsoever to youth in today's world. Perhaps the educator was correct in his indictment.

Our listening, moreover, has to occur in a context of compassion and understanding. Most of us realize that today's young person is almost radically different from his counterpart of our generations, yet a home-grown product, the result at least partially of the frustrations, illusions, hypocrisies, compromises and affluence of his parents' world.

He is a disturbing blend of idealist, iconoclast, rebel, ingrate, dreamer, reformer, seeker and mixed-up kid. He has been hurt by his elders' gross insensitivity to human suffering and injustice, and revolted by their selfish inconsistencies between profession and deed. He is gullible and often doesn't know it—the ready prey of unscrupulous interlopers who would use his idealism for their darker purposes. He is frequently profane and vulgar and the morality he would die for is a morality that sometimes ignores and even shatters conventional sex mores and concentrates on issues like human rights and war. He has handled a mass of knowledge almost infinitely larger than that managed by us in our world; and his intelligence is of a very high order. There are occasions when he is ideologically ready to destroy without having planned how to rebuild, glibly affirming that anything—or even nothing—would be better than the status quo.

He tends to turn you off, often but not always politely, if you are over 30. He is often more opinionated and prejudiced than those he loudly condemns for being that way—but he won't admit it. He is slow to read books that deal thoughtfully with another point of view, nor is he ready to hear willingly addresses or sermons which espouse philosophies he has already dismissed. He plays with Marxism and other radical world views as a kid fools with fireworks—not meaning to get hurt but chancing it for the kicks. He has no racial hang-up and pities those who do. He means to turn this world upside-down and is impatient to get on with the job. It often appears that he couldn't care less about *your* sense of values and commitments —but, in a departure from integrity of which he seems unaware, he seems willing and eager for you and the decadent system you represent to pick up the tab on his revolutionary antics.

He defies freedom, but sometimes it isn't the brand of freedom implicit in Western history. He is often against the institutional church but he isn't against Jesus. He simply can't see very much obvious connection between the two. He is enormously bitter about Vietnam and terribly suspicious of the military and industrial complex which he is pretty sure bears major responsibility for it.

And curious though it seems—his magnificent obsessions and his principled polemics can still be interrupted and even postponed by the kind of gastronomical interlude that provides heaps of hamburgers and french fries and stacks of blueberry pies!

I believe in this young person, deeply and genuinely—not in all that he does and not in all that he wishes me to do: but I believe in him. In my opinion, he is more honest, more devastatingly forthright and more idealistic (although he probably deplores the word) than my generation or any generation I have known.

My first task as a parent, and educator or a churchman is to convey to him this message of my confidence in his essential integrity. In order to do this, I must often be willing to look beyond his appearance, his language and perhaps even his lifestyle and his odor. He knows quickly and sensitively whether I am accepting or rejecting him as an authentic individual, and he cares immensely about this.

This young person (and of course all of my description refers to women as well as men, and my use of "he" is generic) has something of terrific importance to say to those of us who are involved in the leadership of the church. This is partly because he sees our times as they are—and not through the tilted vision of complacent luxury and coddled prejudices. It is also because he has sacrificed gaiety's laughter for compassion's tears and has developed a perspective on life whose grim seriousness represents maturity far beyond his years. He is involved, deeply involved, in the hurt of the world. Again, it is because he seeks to be terribly and ultimately honest, and possesses a shattering power to cut through sham and hypocritical rationales.

Do you recall the words of the woman at the well about the Lord, in John 4, "Come, see a man, which told me all things that ever I did?" If we can hear their voice, youth today, with stern honesty, will fluoroscope the conscience of the church—and in what they reveal may appear our most reliable guidance to its renewal.

Here I insert a somber parenthesis: I think the renewal of the church cannot with integrity be committed to those who despise it and are unwilling themselves to accept the entirety of its gospel. Youth dedicated to reaching the goals of radical and revolutionary change by journeying down paths of willful destruction are hardly safe guides for human society in any age. Young people arrogantly demanding and caustically bitter, deliberately disrupting instead of skillfully building, often shrouding logic in blasphemy—such young people can hardly be said to represent accurately or fairly the throngs of constructively disturbed and even angry young men and women who form the creative nucleus of a generation upon which all humankind pins its hopes for a better tomorrow. Youth's freedom like the freedom of every person has to involve responsibleness. Close of parenthesis!

We Must Undertake What They Think Is Important

Modern young people are interested in a less materialistic society. They are against our preoccupation with, and exploitation of, the thing world. Their emphasis is upon human values. This ought not to disturb the Christian community, for it reproduces the mind of Jesus and represents prophetic insight into one of the critical illnesses of our time.

Again, modern young people, particularly those still within the church, seem to me to be deeply concerned about *a recovery of emphasis on Jesus Christ*. I do not discover that they have turned him off, but rather that they have turned off what we in too many instances have done to him.

One college student, at home for the summer, in spite of his lack of conventional respect for the institutional church, devoted many spare hours to listing and cataloging all the statements of Jesus in the four gospels. If contemporary youth claim any pantheon of heroes at all, surely the Man of Galilee will be prominent among them.

Once more, concerned young people feel it is important *to make an authentic effort to improve life in our country and world*, particularly at the trouble points of war, racism, poverty, population explosion, ecology, etc. They would certainly agree with Dag Hammarskjöld of United Nations fame that "in our day, the road to holiness must necessarily lead through the world of action." Tucked away in a brochure on *Youth in the Seventies* issued by a well-known American industry, in a brief article by the 21-year-old daughter of an employee of that company, was this exciting sentence: "In colonial times the established order was one to be admired: it was composed of the established economic and civic leaders who were also the great revolutionaries and intellects." *Well, why not again?*

What a difference it might conceivably make in the attitude of young people today if those of us who belong to the present Establishment would become deeply and creatively involved in those radical and revolutionary alterations of present patterns in life and society which have to occur before our world can be either humanized or Christianized to any measurable extent. We might do well to ponder the probability that today's power structures and establishments have brought on themselves many of the indictments from which they suffer!

I remember my last visit to old St. John's Church in Richmond, when I stood again where Patrick Henry, the orator of the American Revolution, delivered his immortal speech. He was not only a political and civic leader, a member of the Establishment in his day; he was also *a great revolutionary and intellect!* He was busily and dangerously at work trying to change life for the better!

And, whether we really believe it or not, concerned modern young people, particularly those who live and think within the Christian community, are anxiously eager to see *the church renewed.*

It has always been difficult to get youth to buy the concept of the church for the pure sake of the institution itself. Ornate architecture, the accouterments of a country club, rich budgets focused on selfish objectives, sterile programs designed to leave unchallenged ancient prejudices—these are useless and even immoral merchandise to young people who have read about the radical simplicity of New Testament Christianity and who feel that the mission of the church is to be servant to its Lord and to the humanity for which he died on the cross.

If such as these are among the objectives of modern young people, let me pose a simple question: *What, in God's name, is wrong with them?*

We Must Recover Certain Lost Chords In Our Theology

It might amaze some young people who have dismissed the Christian faith to discover how many of the Bible's basic thrusts actually coincide with their own fundamental concerns.

For example, *the structures of this world are unacceptable to Jesus Christ.* There is this language in Mark 11: "Then they came into Jerusalem, and Jesus went into the temple and began to drive out those who were buying and selling there. He overturned the tables of the money changers and the benches of the dove sellers and he would not allow people to carry their waterpots through the temple. And he taught them and said, 'Doesn't the Scripture say, My house shall be called a house of prayer for all nations? But you have turned it into a thieves' kitchen!'"

And in Matthew 10: "Never think I have come to bring peace upon the earth. No, I am not come to bring peace but a sword!" The blessing of Christianity was not intended to rest in approving benediction upon either capitalism or any other economic or political philosophy, for the Bible never, ever sanctifies any existing order but rather sits in solemn, godly judgment upon them all.

Again, young people are committed to the recreation of their world, and quite clear in the New Testament message is God's promise (expressed in Revelation 21) that *a new heaven and a new earth* shall be indeed realities.

Or, we are *not to destroy this world, but to live in it* for Jesus Christ—a task or mission suggested by the Master in his parable in Luke 19 and put by him cryptically: "Occupy till I come." Surely one of the most important lessons which impatient revolutionaries need to master in our day is the one suggested by Harry Emerson Fosdick when he declared: "All reformation is restoration." *Restoration— not destruction!*

I would record here my own deep conviction that violence on the American campus must be stopped now and that this is the inescapable obligation of concerned students, faculty, administration and trustees. Violence is tragically inimical not only to human life and expensive and indispensable properties, but also to the processes of reason and the stored treasures of research so ineradicably involved in the educational enterprise. In the ashes of the Wisconsin Math Research Center at Madison lie buried not only precious and irreplaceable data but also whatever shaky rationale ever existed for the violent fringe of campus anger.

And, finally, his Kingdom is coming. How hungry are those who live "in the country of the young" for *authentic hope*—hope that shines out like an evening star over Vietnam and all the tortured places of earth where the sinfulness of today's world boils in unrelieved horror.

There is a famous story of Faust gambling with his soul, about which an artist has painted a picture of a game of chess with Faust at one side and Satan at the other. In the picture the game is almost over and Faust has left only a king, a knight and one or two pawns. He wears on his face a look of utter despair, while at the other side of the board the Devil leers in contemplation of his coming triumph. Many a chess player, looking at the picture, has agreed that the position is hopeless —a checkmate. But one day a master of the game stood in the picture gallery gazing at the scene. He was fascinated at Faust's expression of utter despair. Then his gaze went to the pieces on the board and he stared at them absorbed as other people came and went. Then, suddenly, the gallery was startled by a ringing shout: "It is a lie! The king and the knight have another move!" To us who are sons and daughters of the Resurrection Faith, it is a parable of our situation. No matter how hopeless the times may seem to be, the king and the knight do have another move!

In the book of the Prophet Jeremiah, chapter 29, verse 11, is this language: "For I know the thoughts that I think toward you, saith the Lord, thoughts of peace, and not of evil, to give you an unexpected end." To be sure, there is an element of the supernatural about this brand of Biblical eschatology, but we may underestimate the elasticity of youth's mind if we determine too quickly that it is unable to embrace such a faith for the future. As Stewart of Scotland has said: "We cannot be children of the Resurrection and not see all the world bathed in Resurrection light."

Tucked away in the Biblical theology we have so often neglected as a church are chords that sing unforgettably the whole symphony of young people's agonies.

We Must Introduce Our Young People To Jesus Christ

Such a sentence sounds like a period piece in a contemporary Christian sermon. I know, but I know more... Behind the nearly incredible growth of the drug culture in recent years is a sweeping desire on the part of many young people to journey into new territories of consciousness, to push back the frontiers of the mind in daringly bold adventures of expansion. *It has been an ecstatic moment of secular mysticism* when the soul of youth, yearning to shatter the bondage of the hideously imperfect here-and-now, has chosen to roam the shadowy but inviting hinterlands of fairer dreams and lovelier horizons. Conscripted as vehicles for an often psychedelic journey have been a whole series of hallucinogenic narcotics, certain obscurantist Eastern religions, astrology, weird models of the occult, etc. For uncertain reasons, modern youth has overlooked the exciting answer to his or her own questions and quests that could be found in the faith of the parental generation.

Behind youth and alcoholic beverages is often the same type of explanation. In the determined and desperate search for security and relief from fear, a modern young person frequently drinks to find a shortcut somewhere, or as a compensation or escape. But the basic search is for something far, far beyond what can ever be obtained through drugs, alcohol, astrology or strange philosophies.

Young people, with or without their own awareness or acknowledgement, actually are on the trail of *something essentially spiritual in nature*. They know, perhaps better than their elders in this world, that a human being "does not live by bread alone."

Dare we who ourselves have been tormented by the church's theological confusions and its uncertain trumpets, dare we deny that the failure of the community of faith to live by its own religious professions and to relate its message significantly and meaningfully to youth culture, has allowed to develop a *dangerous vacuum* into which alien elements and forces have moved with sure swiftness?

As one modern thinker suggests in current theological idiom, our young people may be actually revolting against *the experience of the absence of God* at this moment in human history, and against an institutional church which has dared to offer itself in place of its Lord and has given a stone when folk have asked for bread!

As one Christian man, I am convinced that the only adequate answer to all the longings and searchings of contemporary youth is to be found in the fullness of the gospel of Jesus Christ. I believe also that the pseudo-sophisticated refusal of the modern church and the modern church-related college or university to entertain this simple but wholly rational proposition is indefensibly short-sighted and represents in some instances an abrogation of their fundamental commitments. To equate such an assertion with brands of fanaticism and fundamentalism would be to do gross injustice not only to this speaker but also to an authentic segment of Christian history.

Some years ago I was a guest at a religious assembly. A young man named John, living there at the same time, had attracted the sympathy of the rest of us because he was a "spastic"—the victim of a peculiar convulsion or spasm of muscles. His body was twisted, his facial muscles were contorted, and the fingers of his restless hands stretched and drew themselves in every direction. One evening rain prevented our going to the great arbor where services were held and we gathered around a ramshackle piano in the lobby of the hotel for a sing. To our amazement and despair someone in the group suggested that John play for us. An almost visible tremor passed through the crowd as he seated himself at the old instrument.

Then came the miracle! Beginning with a medley of old folk tunes, he progressed to familiar hymns and then to music of a more serious type. His twisted back straightened; the lines of his face became relaxed and even beautiful; the nervous contortions of his hands were replaced by a liquid grace that swept up and down the keyboard with skill and artistry. The magic of music had set him free! As we listened breathlessly he played Gershwin's *Rhapsody in Blue*, Schubert's *Serenade*, and Chopin's *Prelude in C Sharp Minor*. It was as though an invisible hand had rested in restraining peace upon his convulsed body.

The glory of the gospel is still that the realized presence of Jesus Christ in the life of a person brings to that individual an even more lyrical freedom than that which came to John at the piano.

So: in my judgment the bridge of fresh communication across the generations cannot be built "in the country of the young" apart from our willingness to listen, to understand and to become deeply and redemptively involved in the radical remaking of human society after the values of the New Testament instead of the materialism implicit in a purely economic interpretation of humankind. And, in the Christian community, this leads ultimately to a transforming encounter with Jesus Christ.

This—as one Christian man sees it—constitutes the only way we can in our day borrow from the ancient wisdom of the Prophet Ezekiel and, *sitting where they sit*, help those who—with us—inhabit "the country of the young" to apply effectively the vision they have seen.

V

Four Sermons Preached
at The Chicago Sunday Evening Club[1]

*The Chicago Sunday Evening Club was founded in 1908 by Clifford W.
Barnes who was its organizational genius and president until his death in
1944. His first desire to have a Sunday night religious program in Chicago's
Loop was not warmly supported by the clergy he contacted, but his second
approach to the Windy City's industrial and commercial leaders met with
overwhelming favor. The meetings were held in Orchestra Hall and this
immense place was filled to capacity until the dawn of the television age.
Those business leaders who succeeded Mr. Barnes, an elite group, recognized
that the new technology had virtually destroyed attendance at such public
services: therefore, they turned to television and began a 30-minute version
of their Sunday night program from Station WTTW, Channel 11. The
Chicago Sunday Evening Club, from the beginning, had made use of the
nation's most distinguished religious leaders for its weekly presentations. This
practice continues until today, although the Club's present program is carried
over the Hallmark Network.*

*I was greatly surprised and completely humbled by the fact that I was
asked to bring messages over a period of years. I recall quite clearly that my
initial inquiry for guidance in what to preach resulted in a recommendation
to be brief (it had to be because of the 30-minute format!), intelligently
simple (no obscure, complex thought), and preferably the choice of a theme
that primarily dealt with aspects of personal religion. All Chicago Sunday
Evening Club sermons are printed in leaflet form and mailed out each week
by the thousands to those who request them.*

*It is the custom of the Chicago Sunday Evening Club to house and feed its
guest ministers at the Chicago Union League Club, a venerable institution
near the Loop which offers luxurious hospitality. In my case, my host at the
telecast who later joined me for dinner at the Union League Club was one of*

the leading executives of Swift International.

I sense no need for an introduction to the first three of the following sermons, but the fourth provided for me such a memorable evening after the telecast that I have undertaken to describe it briefly.

Blessed Be His Name![2]

Text: *"And Jesus answering said, Were there not ten cleansed? But where are the nine?"* (Luke 17:17)

It is both an honor and a privilege to be permitted to stand here, albeit unworthily, in the succession of those who have appeared for the Chicago Sunday Evening Club since its founding in 1907.

"Where are the nine?" These words of our Lord constitute one of the most poignant, plaintive queries in Holy Scripture. Ten had been cleansed, but only one of the ten—a stranger—had returned to give thanks for healing. This striking story points up the lack of gratitude which is such a tragic characteristic of the human race. In our own day, perhaps more than in New Testament times, one of the vanishing virtues seems to be the grace of thankfulness. Have you ever stopped to consider what a difference an effort to be grateful might make in your own life? When I was a college president, I used to feel that if I could get a student to be grateful—grateful to parents, teachers, church, and country—I would be well along the way toward helping him or her to discover solutions for all of his or her problems, academic and otherwise.

Against the backdrop of this ancient, probing question of Jesus, I wish to offer a single Christian man's testimony of thanksgiving. If my meditation had a title, it would be "Blessed be His Name!"

The Ordinary Blessings of Life

First of all, as a Christian man I am grateful for the *ordinary blessings of life*, those things which we so often take for granted.

In an open letter, Robert S. Kreider, a Mennonite, says that to nine-tenths of the earth's people he is fabulously rich. He gives these reasons:

> "I have never been desperately hungry,
> I have never been a refugee,
> I have never been a prisoner,
> The secret police have never knocked on our door at night,
> No lepers roam the streets of our village,
> I have always lived within a few minutes of a doctor's services,
> In our town I have never heard the guns of approaching armies,
> No one died in our community this year of starvation,

Our house has many rooms and each member of our family has a bed."

How easy it is to take basic things for granted! I am thankful for the splash of a raindrop, the gentle warmth of the sunshine, harvest-time, the pristine purity of the snow, the purple royalty of twilight, the shimmering melody of moonlight on the water, the deep, rich symphony of greens in a summer woodland. I am grateful for the presence of music in the world, a truly international language saying for us the unsayable, until we can sense that Holland was right when he declared that music is "a rose-lipped shell murmuring of the eternal sea."

I am grateful for shelter from the elements, strength for the day's toil, worthy goals toward which to strive, institutions like the school and the church to feed the mind and the spirit, and a government to protect our right to be free. I am grateful for the circle of loved ones by my fireside. An individual's true wealth is never computed in terms of his bank account, real estate, stocks and bonds, social influence or political power. It is computed instead in terms of that intimate family circle composed of those who love him best and whom he loves most. Here is his true treasure. Beyond all of this, I am grateful for what I sometimes call "the surprises of God"—unexpected strength in the midst of a hard task, a new friendship to break the spell of loneliness, incredible blessing fashioned out of the very stuff of tragedy. These are the Heavenly Father's precious gifts to his children, hidden through our years much as a mother hides toys throughout the house before a child's birthday. We keep stumbling upon them at the most unexpected places and the most unanticipated moments. They lie wholly beyond our merit and even beyond our highest expectation. They make us live on spiritual tiptoe every day of our lives.

These great fundamental blessings of life are themselves so wonderful as to defy comprehension. Paul, writing in I Corinthians 2:9, reminded us, "Eye hath not seen, nor ear heard, neither have entered into the heart of man, the things which God hath prepared for them that love him." Not all of these things are in Heaven, my friends. Many of them are right here upon this earth, surrounding us from day to day. As a Christian man, I thank God for the great ordinary blessings of life. Blessed be His Name!

Work To Do

Again, as a Christian man, I thank God for *work to do*. No matter how honorable or essential one's means of earning a livelihood may be, it does not constitute the primary reason for his or her existence. The person who has mastered the meaning and mystery of life will always subordinate his or her vocation to the larger proposition that God has some special purpose for that person, and life becomes meaningful only as this purpose is discovered and accomplished.

There is a lovely story about Roland Hayes, the great African American tenor who was the first of our country's artists to be invited to sing before a Russian audience after the Bolshevik Revolution. Standing before a vast throng in the city of Moscow, Mr. Hayes suddenly remembered that his listeners were Communists and did not believe in God. In the same moment he remembered that he was a Christian. He bowed his head in a moment of silent prayer, then sang as he had never sung before "I Know That My Redeemer Lives!" Roland Hayes was a distinguished performing artist, but he was first of all a witnessing Christian.

We are staggered by the immensity of the evil which we see entrenched and malignant all about us. But we are even more amazed by the consciousness that God has planned for us who are his children to be part of the answer to that evil. To realize this truth is enough to give life deep meaning and high, ecstatic romance.

Our contribution to the solution of the problem of wrongdoing in our world does not need to be a large one. Indeed, most of us are not capable of anything spectacular or grandiose or even important, as the world measures importance, at this point. We must content ourselves with modest efforts, but we are strengthened by recognizing that God has made his own arrangements for such efforts to count in a way entirely disproportionate to their own apparent significance. A number of years ago a London chambermaid one Sunday morning handed some verses to her pastor at Westminster Chapel, the late Dr. G. Campbell Morgan. These are the lines which Dr. Morgan read:

> "Lord of all pots and pans and things,
> Since I've no time to be
> A saint by doing lovely things,
> Or watching late with Thee,
> Or dreaming in the dawnlight,
> Or storming heaven's gates,
> Make me a saint by getting meals
> And washing up the plates.

> "Although I must have Martha's hands,
> I have a Mary mind;
> And when I black the boots and shoes,
> Thy sandals, Lord, I find.
> I think of how they trod the earth,
> What time I scrub the floor—
> Accept this meditation, Lord,
> I haven't time for more.

"Warm all the kitchen with Thy love,
   And light it with Thy peace;
Forgive me all my worrying,
   And make all grumbling cease;
Thou who didst love to give men food
   In room or by the sea,
Accept this service that I do—
   I do it unto Thee."[1]

When we undertake to do our Father's work in the world, no matter how small the task, God touches it with Heaven's power and gives it meaning and influence in the whole sequence of human events! As a Christian man, I thank God today for work to do. Blessed be His Name!

The Hope of The Future

As a Christian man, I thank God for *the hope of the future*. Mr. Norman Cousins has reminded us that during the last 3,200 years humankind has entered into 4,711 treaties, of which 4,697 have been broken. How difficult it is to justify speaking of hope in a world where the horror of Vietnam still lingers, and the dismal danger of the Middle East hovers like a cloud over distraught humanity. Christian people are the only authentically hopeful people on the face of the earth today. In both of God's Covenants with his people, the Old and the New, it is promised that righteousness will triumph in the affairs of humans. The thrilling assurance of our Christian Faith, given again and yet again, is that truth crushed to earth will rise again, the eternal years of God are hers!

The Christian believes emphatically in a philosophy of history. He or she believes that history is what E. Stanley Jones years ago said it was, "His-story." He has supreme and unshakable confidence that an omnipotent God is busy behind the scenes of human events, bringing to pass his will and way in his own good time.

It is this kind of faith which produces courage to face difficulty, serenity to live in the midst of turmoil. *When a man's or a woman's convictions go down deeper than that person's fears, nothing that life can ever do to him or her will hurt very much.* As a Christian man, I thank God for the hope of the future. Blessed be His Name!

The Gospel

Finally, as a Christian man, I thank God for *the gospel*. Edwin Arlington Robinson, in one of his last essays, said our world is a kind of spiritual kindergarten in which millions of bewildered infants are trying to spell out God with the wrong building blocks. Perhaps so, but it doesn't need to be. We have the gospel. We had it as a gentle suggestion in the pages of the Old Testament, as in Isaiah 1:18, "Come now, and let us reason together, saith the Lord: though your sins be as scarlet, they shall be white as snow; though they be red like crimson, they shall be as wool." The suggestion became the crescendo of a tremendous affirmation in the New Testament, John 3:16, "For God so loved the world that he gave his only begotten Son, that whosoever believeth in him should not perish, but have everlasting life."

When the Everlasting God planned a nearer visit to earth, he chose the utterly human trails of a mother's deep anguish and a baby's low, helpless cry for the Divine pilgrimage. He might have come as a heavenly visitant in trappings of cosmic splendor with spirit-legions and a chariot made of the winds! But he elected instead a cattle shelter and the loneliness of a man and a woman. This is the meaning of the Incarnation, the message of every preacher and the wonder of the church's Good News.

God himself stood over the manger cradle, over the wilderness years, over the brief and fleeting period of Jesus' earthly ministry, over the trials, over the Cross of Golgotha, over the empty tomb of Joseph, stood over them all and cried out in tones broken with love indescribable "and thereto I plight thee my troth!"

My faith is not in creeds, as important as I know accurate theology to be. My faith is not in the church, as much as I love it and believe in it. My faith is in a Person, Jesus Christ, Son of God and Son of Man, the fairest among ten thousand, the One altogether lovely, Emmanuel—God with us! It was of him that the gentle Gypsy Smith in his inimitable way, said, "He is the jewel for which the rest of this vast universe is but a setting."

We have the gospel, the message of God's illimitable love for lost men and lost women. There comes a time when in our weariness and despair, we need to lean back upon Everlasting Arms and let the glory and wonder of God's promises saturate our souls with fresh hope and new courage. It is the miracle of Christianity that no man, no woman is ever beyond the power of this gospel to save and to restore. As a Christian man, I thank God today for the gospel. Blessed be His Name!

"But where are the nine?"! Where, indeed, are they? We used to sing a song we do not use very much anymore, a song which tells us:

> "Count your many blessings, name them one by one;
> And it will surprise you what the Lord hath done."

Have you ever stopped to consider what the recovery of gratitude could do for your life? Your marriage? Your business or profession? Your relations with kinspeople and neighbors? Your own happiness and contentment? I *dare* you, I dare *you* to go out into this new week and be grateful in the secret places of your soul!

In the name of the Father, Son, and Holy Spirit. Amen.

A Believer's Insights³

Texts: *"...hope maketh not ashamed..."* (Romans 5:5a)
   "...if it were not so, I would have told you..." (John 14:2)

We have heard many times that "it's all in the way you look at it." This is particularly true in the Christian community. A person who knows Jesus Christ has a way of looking at life which is utterly, even radically, different from the manner in which another person looks at it. He or she long since has discovered that "hope maketh not ashamed." This transcendently different conviction is supported by the very integrity of God as Jesus himself suggested: "If it were not so, I would have told you."

Let me, then, explore with you three different perspectives which compose at least the beginning of a believer's insights.

I.

We are to believe not the worst but the best. A modern person, shoved into the quagmire of an almost completely secularized society, has some honest and searching questions:

1.   Does life make sense? Is it a tale told by an idiot, or is it a tapestry woven by the sensitive fingers of God?
2.   Is there a genuine idealism possible in human relations, or is this theory an unrealistic dodging of the ugly facts of human nature?
3.   Dare we actually believe that the divine, creative Spirit of the universe is concerned about us as individuals?
4.   Is there any dependable reason to look beyond the near shoreline of international slaughter, mass suffering and torture and tyrannical oppression to a more distant horizon of peace, human charity and liberty?

These queries arise out of the very nature of our times: ideas, habits, conventions, institutions, ethical and moral standards are all as "frail as frost landscapes on a window pane." Do you remember the words of the Angel Gabriel to De Lawd in Mark Connelly's play *Green Pastures*? "Everything nailed down is a-comin' loose!" This is a cryptic, staccato description of our times, characterized by frightening accuracy. A massive bewilderment has permeated all of our thought and action, even the realm of religion. The little girl who became mixed up in her recital spoke for many of us when she said,

> "Twinkle, twinkle, little star;
> How I wonder what I are."

But over against all of our dismal futility and our brittle doubting is the gospel. In Ephesians 2:10 we read, "For we are his workmanship created in Christ Jesus unto good works..." "Workmanship" in Greek is the same word from which we get our word "poem." What is being said in this verse is quite audacious: when a person receives Jesus Christ as Savior and Lord, he or she becomes, in very fact, God's poem, the Divine dream "created in Christ Jesus unto good works." This is a radically different idea about a human being from that which is commonly held in our time. The greatest of all the dangers of *Playboy Magazine* is its low anthropology, its insistence that a human being is a brilliantly cultivated brain to be used, enjoyed and often exploited by another human being. This brand of anthropology is totally horizontal, and the idea that a human has any relationship whatsoever to another world or to Someone beyond himself or herself is wholly missing.

The incredible inroads in our thinking and acting made by the moral revolution in recent years, I propose, are traceable in large measure to such a horizontal anthropology. If life as we know it is ultimately concluded by the experience of death, if there is no Supreme Being to whom a human is accountable for his or her thoughts, words and deeds, then it is understandable how very many people would insist that moral and ethical consequences simply do not exist. But if, on the other hand, a human being is a creature of eternity, made to live forever, answerable to God for his or her deeds in the flesh—one for whom the Son of God died upon a Cross, then everything is vastly and sweepingly different! I can see no way to restore in human society in our time a sense of moral sanity and integrity apart from a thorough-going re-discovery of the Biblical doctrine of persons. We find this doctrine stated in many places in Holy Scripture, but nowhere more vividly than the articulation given it by the author of the 8th Psalm: "What is man that thou art mindful of him, and the son of man that thou visitest him? For thou hast made him a little lower than the angels, and hast crowned him with glory and honor." (Psalm 8:4–5). Have you ever wondered why the Psalmist elected to say "a little lower than the angels" instead of "a little higher than the animals?" I think the answer is quite simple: man's frame of reference was always intended to be in heaven, and not upon earth! *We are to think not the worst but the best about human beings!*

When we do this, our total perspective upon life is transformed. We suddenly realize that concern, mercy, righteousness and redemption are the magnificent obsessions at the heart of the universe—and in the heart of God. Do you remember the moment in *A Pilgrim's Progress* when Pilgrim's guide called back from the midst of the swirling waters, "Be of good cheer, my brother, for my feet have touched the bottom and it is sound?" We are privileged, as believers, to regard the foundation of life, in spite of suffering and tragedy, as being sound. Sewers are real, but so are mountain brooks. Judas Iscariot was real, but so, bless God, is Jesus Christ! How we need a generation of poets, novelists and dramatists willing to write about life from this viewpoint!

This is a believer's insight: we are to think not the worst but the best. As Peter Marshall once put it, "In our Heavenly Father's world, there are some things too good *not* to be true!"

II.

The only ultimate answer to humanity's problem is spiritual. No generation has ever been so nearly suffocated by a plethora of problems as has ours. Someone brought me a slogan for my desk which read, "If you can keep calm under the present circumstances—you simply don't understand the situation!"

I know the multiplied social diseases that imperil humanity, as do you: racism, hatred, violence, poverty, war, the ecological danger, etc. *I believe that these problems are part of the business of the Christian Church.* I am grateful for every good law which has been passed in the legislative bodies of the world propelling humanity a little nearer to practices of justice and righteousness. But I also believe that effective and permanent social action must be grounded in a re-discovery of God's Word, in a sound theology, and in an authentic experience of Jesus Christ.

I have become convinced that we cannot expect a generation of men and women fundamentally insensitive to the person and claims of Jesus Christ to remain for very long willing to support and sustain his principles in human affairs. A distinguished preacher of recent years put it quaintly when he said, "You cannot stir up a dozen rotten eggs and expect to get a decent omelet!" Therefore, quite beyond the legitimate functions of prophecy and protest, *the basic business of the Christian Church is still to enable God to make us into new human beings.* That curious contemporary poet e. e. cummings had a bit of prose which haunted me when I first read it, and haunts me still: "Better worlds are born, not made, and their birthdays are the birthdays of individuals."

Rugged Thomas Carlyle in one of his essays declared that a person who goes out to rent a room should not inquire of his prospective landlady what the price of the room will be. Rather, said Carlyle, he should inquire what she thinks about God. If her thinking about God is right, then the price of the room will be fair! This may be a principle which the modern church has forgotten to its own detriment. What I am saying is simply this: we have been looking too often in the wrong places for solutions to our problems. A believer knows that the only ultimate answer to the issues which torment humanity is a spiritual answer!

III.

Let me propose my third insight, and my best one. A believer knows that *God keeps his promises!*

Implicit in the Old Covenant was the promise of a New Covenant. The Hebrew Scriptures are alternately bold vision and anxious sigh. It was a long, long time to wait. The Jewish people wondered, even as they rebuked themselves for wondering, if God would keep his promise.

Then, in the simple magnificence of Paul's language in Galatians 4:4, "When the *fullness of the time was come,* God sent forth his Son...." God had, indeed, kept his promise—his greatest promise! The most exciting awareness that can ever break over the consciousness of a Christian is the realization that God *always* keeps his promises, and that the very integrity of his own character guarantees this. "If it were not so," said Jesus, "I would have told you."

The promises of God run like a silken cord around the whole package of Scriptures:

> "Come now, and let us reason together, saith the Lord, though your sins be as scarlet, they shall be as white as snow; though they be red like crimson, they shall be as wool" (Isaiah 1:18).

This is a promise of God!

> "I have loved thee with an everlasting love..." (Jeremiah 31:3).

This is another promise of God.

> "My grace is sufficient for thee: for my strength is made perfect in weakness" (II Corinthians 12:9a).

This is his assurance to us.

> "I will never leave thee nor forsake thee" (Hebrews 13:5).

This also is his promise.

> "I am the resurrection, and the life: he that believeth in me, though he were dead, yet shall he live: and whosoever liveth and believeth in me shall never die. Believest thou this?" (John 11:25-26).

This, blessed be his name, is his promise!

> "For the earth shall be filled with the knowledge of the glory of the Lord, as

the waters cover the sea" (Habakkuk 2:3).

"And I, if I be lifted up from the earth, will draw all men unto me" (John 12:32).

and

"The kingdoms of the world are become the kingdoms of our Lord, and of his Christ; and he shall reign forever and ever" (Revelation 11:15b).

These, too, are his promises!

Do you remember the lovely Advent passage in Isaiah 52, verse 7?
"How beautiful upon the mountains are the feet of him who brings good tidings, who publishes peace, who brings good tidings of good, who publishes salvation, who says to Zion, 'Your God reigns.'"

Have you ever examined the imagery of this passage? It suggests a deep mountain valley at dawning. Have you been there? All around you the night lingered, its darkness penetrated only by a silver sliver of light which filtered through the treetops like a slender finger of God Himself. But looking upward to the mountaintop, you saw there the golden glory of a sunrise that had not yet come to your valley. Its beauty sang an anthem of hope and joy for your soul. In the valley there was the gloom of darkness, but on the mountaintop the wonder of a new morning! "How beautiful upon the mountains are the feet of him who brings good tidings..." This is the gospel, this is God's promise, guaranteed by the integrity of Heaven itself!

Many years ago I saw a motion picture in which Will Rogers starred. Its final scene is etched upon my memory. Mr. Rogers played the role of an old tramp, and in the last moments of the picture, wearing a tattered suit and a disreputable old hat, his hands thrust into his pockets, he walked away from camera, singing as he went, "There's a great day a-coming, there's a great day a-coming..." Every Christian believes this. There *is* a great day coming, for us as individuals who have faith in Jesus Christ, for human society and for history itself—because of the death and resurrection of our Lord Jesus Christ. *God keeps his promises*! If we can believe this, really believe it, it can revolutionize our lives during the days of a new week.

I have been speaking today of *fundamental things*, matters which in our easy contemporary sophistication we are prone to overlook. It is, indeed, all in the way a person views life. "Hope maketh not ashamed." Perhaps the church needs more than anything else to discover these fundamental, rudimentary things again.

I give you a simple story. Gilbert Keith Chesterton, the brilliant British essayist, had a monumental mind but an incredibly short memory. One day he left his home for a speaking engagement, but en route forgot where he was to appear that night.

He sent a telegram to his wife with these words, "Am in Market Harborough. Where ought I to be?" She sent back a wire of a single word: "Home!" Then she said to a neighbor that she felt if she could get the old fool home, it would be easier to start him out in a different direction then it would be to get him from where he was to where he was supposed to be! I am convinced that this same thing is true of the church in our time. Perhaps we need to come home again to the *basics* of the Christian gospel, and then set out in a better direction. This would be easier to accomplish than an attempt to get us from where we are to where we ought to be!

I have spoken of a believer's insights—those things that are different because of faith in Christ. What I have said has to do with the mystery, the wonder, the glory and the joy of the Christian gospel—*and* the radical transformation it produces in a person's perspective on life. May you experience a new understanding of these truths through the power of God's Spirit.

In the name of the Father, Son, and Holy Spirit. Amen.

The Highway to God[4]

Text: *"And ye shall seek me and find me when ye shall search for me with all your heart."* Jeremiah 29:13

I am deeply convinced with the conviction that there are those listening today who need religion's *basic message*—that upon which all others depend. They need God. It is possible to be members of a church, even officers in it, and yet to miss this pearl of greatest price. Therefore, I am speaking primarily to that man or woman who needs to turn his or her footsteps down the highway that leads to God.

Let me make a startling statement. No person on the face of the earth today, no matter who he or she may be and no matter what that person may have been guilty of doing is more than *four steps away from God.*

A Sense of Need

The first of these steps is what I would call a sense of need. No one can be helped until he or she realizes that help is needed. The person who has determined to go forward in his or her own strength is alienated from those streams of assistance that flow out from the throne of God. Self-satisfaction, self-complacency is the key that effectively bars the door of the human heart. This is what Jesus was talking about when he gave us the parable of the Pharisee and the Publican. "And he spake also this parable unto certain which *trusted in themselves...*" You may remember that it was the Pharisee who stood outside the gates of God's joy because he felt no need. It was the Publican who was overwhelmed with a sense of sin, who prayed "God, be merciful to me a sinner," and who received the grace of God.

Feeling your need for God is the first step in the preparation of your mind and heart to receive him. This is not only good religion; it is sound psychology as well.

There are certain things which we can do to help God create this sense of need within us. In the first place, we can *look at ourselves.* "Know thyself," said the wise philosopher. "Oh, wad some power the giftie gie us to see oursilves as ithers see us!" sang Bobby Burns. We need to examine our lives—not just the living rooms and the libraries, but the attics, the cellars, and all the hidden closets about which only we know. We need to see the darkened corners, checkered with cobwebs and littered with trash. We need to be open, frank and devastatingly brutal in our self-analysis. But we dare not stop here: we must move on to *look at Jesus*, for he is God to us, the revelation of the Divine Spirit at the center of the universe. And he is perfect, he who said, "Be ye therefore perfect, even as your Father which is in heaven is perfect." Measured by that standard, everyone of us must acknowledge his sinfulness and his nothingness. It is as though a brilliant, lustrous diamond from some fabulous imperial crown were placed alongside a pitiful, artificial jewel of paste; or as though a priceless canvas from the brush of a Rembrandt were posed with a cheap print from a ten-cent counter; or as though the great surging music of a Beethoven or a Handel were played on the same program with the brittle, tawdry tunes of our times. When a person sees himself or herself beneath the revealing incandescence of Christ's holy will, the only cry that can escape those tortured lips is the exclamation by one of long ago, "Woe is me, Lord, for I am undone!" We see ourselves as we are, we sense our desperate need, and we understand that Saint Augustine was everlastingly right when centuries ago he said, "Thou hast made us for Thyself, O Lord, and our spirits are restless until they rest in Thee." This is the beginning of salvation—the first step along the highway to God.

> "Let not conscience make you linger,
> Nor of fitness fondly dream;
> All the fitness He requireth
> Is to feel your need of Him."

Repentance

The second step on the highway to God is the step of *repentance*. Now, repentance presupposes sin, and the blasé pride of our fickle generation has been too sophisticated to acknowledge that sin is real—particularly the sin in our own lives. The process of *rationalizing away* a guilt feeling is the cleverest and best device the Devil has. We dare not trust our own minds at this point, for the moment we do an evil thing, our minds rush to save our faces. We justify ourselves. But over all of this, and under and through it all, there is still the hideous, horrible fact of sin. Ibsen called it a ghost that haunts a man. George Eliot in *Adam Bede* said "sin is like a bit of poor workmanship, there's no end to the mischief it'll do," and Christopher Morley referred to it as "those terrible impediments that rest upon the soul." Sin is still the curse of the human race, and there is a sense in which there is just as much of it in our refined and beautiful sanctuaries of religion as there is in the roughest rescue mission on New York's East Side. No man, no woman can get to God while sin is in the way. There must be repentance, and repentance is first of all *confession*, taking the skeleton out of the closet. I like this illustration: When some impurity gets into drinking water or milk, the careful, cautious housewife sets it on the stove and *boils the poison out*. Confessing one's sins is "boiling the poison out," releasing the disease that holds one's mind in its awful bondage. The burden of a sin unconfessed is a brace that shackles the soul. It throws life off-center and leads to disaster.

But repentance is more than mere confession. There must also be a *moral disavowal of sin*. A person must hate sin enough to abandon it, not for a season, but forever. The trouble with so many well-intentioned people who are trying to live Christian lives today is that there has never been a final decree of divorcement between them and their sins, but only a temporary separation which has led at last to a fatal reunion. There must be a moral disavowal which says NO to sin FOREVER. When there is added to this formula of confession and moral disavowal the willingness to make restitution for one's wrongdoing, in so far as it is possible, regardless of the cost, then a person may be said to have repented and his voice may be blended legitimately with the chorus of those who sing:

"My Jesus, I love Thee, I know Thou art mine,
For Thee all the follies of sin I resign."

Consecration

The third step on the highway that leads to God is the step of *consecration*. This follows repentance logically as well as chronologically. Repentance is the laying of the bad things of life at the foot of the Cross; consecration is the laying of all things there. The wise men brought to the Infant Savior their gifts of gold and frankincense and myrrh. The gold represented their material possessions; the frankincense represented their deepest longings and aspirations, the dreams of their souls; the myrrh represented their lives, their sufferings, and if need be their deaths. They brought everything they had and placed it at the feet of the Christ. No person can enter into a full relationship with God until a full surrender of life has been made—this is the law of reciprocity in the economy of Grace! Many a person is missing the blessings of Christian joy because there is some area of his life or her life which has not been yielded to the Lord. It may be an individual's wrong attitudes toward people of other races, it may be a person's insensitive acceptance of the privileges of affluence in a world poverty-stricken and famine-ridden. It may be a person's way of treating his or her family, or paying the family debts, or running a business or practicing a profession, or filling out an income tax report. It could be sex. Peter Marshall reminded us that sex will either be the nastiest or the nicest thing in our lives. If there is *any* area of life that has not been totally surrendered to God, then an individual has not yet taken the third step that leads down the highway to God.

Faith

The last, best step on the highway to God is the step of *faith*. This is trusting God to do his part when we are perfectly sure that we have done ours. To the person who has felt a need, who has repented, who has made a full consecration of life, our God brings his priceless gift of salvation and life abundant and eternal. "This is a faithful saying, worthy of all acceptation, that Christ Jesus came into the world to save sinners" (I Timothy 1:15). It is not enough to repent or to consecrate oneself—these acts alone may be ethical acts and religion is vastly more than ethics. There must be that final act when we accept what Jesus Christ has done for us and receive the life of God, his nature and his love, into our hearts by faith—it is this that transforms ethics into love and sets the heart of the universe aquiver with the throb of redemption. This Christian life in the end is a *love relationship*, a personal tryst between a human being and God, begun when we receive his cleansing power and love into our lives by faith. It is a splendid fact that you can take this final step on the highway that leads to God whenever you are willing to do it.

When I was a university student, I remember hearing Dr. S. D. Gordon, who wrote the wonderful series of books entitled *Quiet Talks*, give an address to the student body. When he had finished, Dr. Gordon leaned over the podium and said, "Now, young ladies and young gentlemen, I want you to close your eyes and bow your heads, and while every head is bowed and every eye closed I want to lead us in prayer." And then he prayed the strangest prayer I ever heard. He did not talk to God at all, but kept right on talking to us. He said, "Now, young ladies and young gentlemen, with your eyes closed and your heads bowed, can you look up in your minds' eyes and see God bending over the balustrades of Heaven in your direction? Do you see him? Ah, there he is, there he is. And now, young ladies and young gentlemen, can you begin to reach the hands of your hearts up in the direction of God's hand reaching down toward you? You're doing it, aren't you? But you can't quite reach God's fingers, can you? Ah, did you see what he did? God just bent a little lower, and now, now you can reach the fingers of God with your fingers. And now you're closing your fingers around his hand. He has you, and you have him—and that's what it means to be a Christian. Amen." It was the most curious prayer I ever heard. But it was the gospel. The last best step on the highway to God is the step of faith. No man, no woman anywhere in the world, no matter who that person is or what that person has done is more than four steps away from God. This is the gospel, this is the rudimentary gospel.

You can depend upon God in a world of broken principles and shattered ideals, you can depend upon God. Years ago the late Dr. Roy L. Smith told a lovely story about a dear old couple who lived alone in a modest cottage on a tiny island in Lake Michigan, not far from the Windy City. They had no neighbors. They were friends of the Smith family and the Smiths agonized over the peril that threatened this couple as their years advanced. One day they had a council of love and decided to invite the old man and his wife to spend the rest of their days as guests in the

Smith household. The next morning Dr. Smith and his daughter went by boat to the island where the old couple lived by themselves. After the amenities had been observed, as tactfully as he could Dr. Smith broached the purpose of their visit and extended the invitation. The old couple heard him through and then the old man turned to his sweetheart of the lengthening years and said, "Of course, we can't accept the invitation, can we, dear?" Dr. Smith began to remonstrate and restate his case, but the old man held up his hand for silence. "Roy," he said, "you simply don't understand; come and we'll show you." Then the old couple, arm in arm, lead the Smiths out of the house, through the yard, and along a winding pathway into the island wilderness until at last they came to a small clearing with a carpet of green grass and a border of beautiful flowers. In the center of this little clearing was a tiny mound with a snow-white cross at its head. The old man put his arm around his wife, and then very quietly said, "We can't leave our island home, for you see we lost a son here." And so, my dear friends, no matter what happens, God can never leave this floating island in his skies because, you see, He lost a Son here! *You can depend upon God.* When everything else collapses and fails you can depend upon him.

Conclusion

There is something more important than beautiful and handsome faces, than bank accounts and real estate and stocks and bonds, than college and university degrees, than political influence and social graces, there is something vastly more important than all of these. Have you, have I, struck hands with the living God? This is the gospel. This is what it is all about. And this is where it all begins. This is forever the major task of the church.

In the name of the Father, Son, and Holy Spirit. Amen.

The Heart Hath Reasons

At the close of the telecast of this sermon, a special group joined me for dinner at the Union League Club. They were my television host and Dr. Kenneth Kantzer, editor of Christianity Today, and Mr. and Mrs. Clarence Blocher from Wheaten, Illinois. Mrs. Blocher, the former Miss Ann King, was a dear friend of ours from high school days and one of the organizers of the Johnson City Youth Council referred to in the final chapter of this book.

I remember that evening for a number of reasons. The food was delicious, the fellowship was warm and affectionately supportive, and the conversation was (to say the least) stimulating. It was good to have opportunity to renew a meaningful friendship with the Blochers, but the exposure to Dr. Kantzer's brilliant and well-informed mind, as he led in the discussion of a variety of topics related to the contemporary church, was something never to be forgotten by me.

It should be said that we always had a coterie of welcome guests at these telecasts, usually composed of Chicago's business leaders who were interested in the Sunday Evening Club. Occasionally two or three would join me for my post-telecast dinner at the Union League Club, but those who came on this particular night were an exceptional and memorable group.

The Heart Hath Reasons[5]

Texts: *"We love him because he first loved us."* I John 4:19
  "The heart hath reasons that the reason knows not of..."
  Blaise Pascal, 17th Century French Scientist and Saint.

When a minister asks for a deeper dedication on the part of his hearers, he usually bases his request upon the need of the world, the challenge of the church or the nature of Christian faith. When these weighty arguments are properly marshaled before the tribunal of reason, the verdict returned ought to be in favor of a more ardent allegiance to the Lord. However, they do not mention the basic fact which actually explains the immortal power of the Christian church. In the universe of a spiritual God there are pleas more compelling, more convincing than the forces of logic and reason can ever be. "The heart hath reasons that the reason knows not of..." Let me illustrate.

This is so when a sensitive spirit is confronted by an *overwhelming idea*. When Alfred Tennyson wrote his exquisite tribute to the memory of Arthur Hallam, which we have in the beautiful poem *In Memoriam*, he could have become enmeshed in a confusion of poetic mechanics: iambic feet, trochaic feet, strophes, sonnets, versification, rhyme. He had to be the master of all these. But beyond them, there was the lyrical devotion of a human being to his friend, which caused the phrases to tumble over each other in sobbing beauty as he sought to express an overwhelming idea:

> "He passed, a soul of nobler tone;
> My spirit loved, and loves him still."

"The heart hath reasons that the reason knows not of..."

It is likewise so in the warmly human sphere of romantic love. I was on a plane recently when seated across from me was a beautiful and charming young lady wearing one of the largest and most brilliant diamonds I have ever encountered. All of us sitting around her could see it, because with a kind of modest immodesty she arranged her hand so that we might have that privilege. As we flew along, she kept casting demure glances of pride and glory in its direction. I pondered the situation. I know what a diamond is—at least I know what the dictionary says it is: "a diamond is a native carbon crystallized in the isometric system, which when cut for jewelry purposes possesses refractive and dispersive powers that are very high, and shows a remarkable brilliancy and play of prismatic coloration." That, dear ladies, is a diamond! But it wasn't *her* diamond. Her diamond was a moonrise over a silver sheet of water, the pale light of stars in the heavens, a mountain brook laughing its way among the rocks, the melody of distant music, the light in her lover's eyes and the lilt in his voice. She was in love, and the poetry of her love sang its way into our souls as we journeyed. "The heart hath reasons that the reason knows not of..."

It is also true in that ultimate earthly experience which we call death. I know, of course, that the Christian's basis for believing in Life Eternal is the Resurrection of Jesus Christ. I know also that fascinating scientific and parascientific discoveries in recent years seem to be pointing to more tangible evidence that there is life beyond the grave. I refer to the famous J. B. Rhyne experiments in extrasensory perception at Duke University, and also to the observations of Dr. Kubler-Ross, Dr. Moody and, more recently, Dr. Maurice Rawlings. I am grateful for all of these exciting explorations. But, as a sensitive human being, I have been aware again and again—as surely have you—that there is still another argument for life beyond the grave. Dr. Fosdick called it "the soul's invincible surmise," and meant by it that interior impulse which wells up within an individual when he or she, standing beside an open grave, becomes conscious of a surpassing reality, namely that death simply cannot contain a person too good and too beloved to die! John Greenleaf Whittier, the Quaker poet, said it beautifully in his "Snowbound:"

> "Who hath not felt in hours of faith
> The truth to flesh and sense unknown,
> That life is ever lord of death,
> And love can never lose its own!"

"The heart hath reasons that the reason knows not of..."

Let us move now into the realm of theological thought and return to our first text: "We love him because he first loved us." If a minister, pleading for deeper dedication, secures an affirmative response from his hearers, it will not be, in the final analysis, because of the need of the world or the challenge of the church or even the nature of the Christian faith. It will be because those hearers realize, in the wonderful words which Jeremiah heard from the Lord, that they have been "loved with an everlasting love," and have made reciprocal response out of hearts awe-stricken with gratitude and gladness. Robert Murray McCheyne, the great Scottish preacher who lived so briefly and served so splendidly at St. Peter's in Dundee, had a beautiful sentence in one of his sermons: "When the summer sun falls full down upon the sea, it draws the vapors upward toward the skies; so, when the sunbeams from the Son of Righteousness fall upon the soul, they draw the constant risings of our love to Him in return." One of the greatest of all Biblical truths is that God has assumed the initiative in seeking and loving his lost children.

This is all a part of the old, old story of the Cross. Canon Burton Streeter said years ago, "The Cross must either be the darkest spot of all in the mystery of existence or else it must be the searchlight by the aid of which we are able to penetrate the surrounding gloom." The Cross is at the center of our Holy Faith, the place where human sin and Divine love meet each other in the greatest of Armageddons. Without attempting to explain the ultimate mystery of the Cross, let me try to say a fresh thing about it just now. I propose that the Cross was a *translation into terms of history of an eternal fact.*

That fact is suggested for us in the magnificent metaphor found in Revelation 7:16 where John of Patmos speaks of "the Lamb in the midst of the throne." We think of God's justice and righteousness, his purity and power, his majesty and glory—and well we may. But the message of this metaphor is that we must also think of his kindness, his love, his compassion, his everlasting mercy—"the Lamb *in the midst of* the throne."

God's great plan of redemption for the human family did not begin at Calvary. Many Scriptures testify to this. In John 8, our Lord says, "Before Abraham was, I am." And again in John 17: "Glorify thou me with the glory which I had with thee *before the world began.*" The author of Hebrews has this same idea in the 13th chapter and the 20th verse: "Now the God of peace, that brought again from the dead our Lord Jesus, that great shepherd of the sheep, through the blood of the *everlasting covenant....*" The beautiful murmur of God's redeeming love which is heard through all the pages of the Old Testament breaks into the crescendo of a mighty shout in the New Testament, at Calvary. The Cross is a translation into terms of history of an *eternal* fact!

Of course, it is certainly more than just that. Christians and theologians have tried to explain its deep meaning through the centuries. They have devised a number of theories to accomplish this: the *ransom* theory, the *satisfaction* theory (offered by Anselm of Canterbury), the *substitution* theory, and the *Governmental* theory (proclaimed by Hugo Grotius). Undoubtedly each of these theories has a part of the truth in it, but no one of them has it all. The Cross is vastly bigger than all that men and women have ever said about it. It towers in magnificent mystery above creeds and theologies. To say that one wholly comprehends its meaning is surely to dim its glory and wonder. As Professor Findley put it so well, "Some great supernatural deed was accomplished by the Cross"—and this deed with its cosmic dimensions dealt forever with human sin, even yours and mine! We do not have to understand in any complete manner the splendid but involved theology of the Cross; multiplied thousands have been saved who have never understood, but have simply laid trusting hold upon its power!

> "Nothing in my hand I bring,
> Simply to Thy Cross I cling!"

Principal P. T. Forsyth, famous British Christian, spoke a very sobering word about the plight of contemporary Christianity when he uttered this sentence: "Our churches are filled with nice, kindly people who have never known the soul's despair or its breathless gratitude." At the heart of the Christian experience is the awareness that our sins have been forgiven, not easily or lightly but at indescribable cost. To have known the terror of sin is to have felt the soul's despair. To have realized that "while we were yet sinners, Christ died for us" is to have experienced the soul's breathless gratitude. There is vast and nearly unbelievable regenerative power in a great forgiveness. To have our churches filled with men and women and young people who have known the joy of release from guilt and the power of sin is to have available for the many thrusts of Christian mission human reserves who do not have to be persuaded to do their religious duty but who are gladly ready for what Kierkegaard called "an endless striving born of gratitude." They know the truth of our text: "We love him because he first loved us." The glory of their lives, their supreme happiness, is to return at least some measure of that love in sacrificial service.

And so what happened on the Cross becomes our motivation. We see what God did for us. Norman Macleod in his *Reminiscences of a Highland Parish* tells an unforgettable story. Many years ago a Highland widow, unable to pay her rent, was threatened with eviction. She set out with her only child to walk across a mountain in order to seek sanctuary in the home of a relative. When she started, the weather was good, but in the mountains she and her baby encountered unexpectedly a terrible snowstorm and did not reach their destination. The next day strong men started to search for her. At the summit of the pass where the storm had been the fiercest they found her frozen in death. Nearby, in the cleft of a sheltering rock, they found her child, safe and well, wrapped in the garments the mother had taken from her own body. Years afterward the son of the minister who had conducted the mother's funeral went to Glasgow to preach a preparatory sermon. The night of the service was stormy and the audience quite small. The snow outside the church reminded the young minister of the story which he had heard so often from his father's lips. He abandoned his prepared manuscript and told his tiny congregation, in simple but eloquent words, the story of a mother's love. A week later he was summoned to the bedside of a dying man whom he did not know. The man seized the minister's hand and said, "Domine, a week ago I stepped into the church where you were preaching to find shelter from the blizzard outside. I had not been to church for many years. I heard you tell the story of a mother's love that night. I wanted you to know that I was the baby who lived because my mother gave her life for me. Often across the years I have thought of that and been grateful for it, but never until I heard you tell the story did I see in what my mother did a picture of what God has done for me through Jesus Christ. I wanted to tell you this and to let you know that my mother's prayers have now been answered."

Do you remember the song which Jenny Lind sang in Royal Albert Hall in London many years ago?

> "There is a green hill far away,
> Without a city wall,
> Where the dear Lord was crucified,
> Who died to save us all.
>
> "We may not know, we cannot tell
> What pains He had to bear,
> But we believe it was for us
> He hung and suffered there.
>
> "There was no other good enough
> To pay the price of sin;
> He only could unlock the gate
> Of Heaven, and let us in.
>
> "He died that we might be forgiven,
> He died to make us good,
> That we might go at last to heaven
> Saved by His precious blood.
>
> "O dearly, dearly has He loved,
> And we must love Him too,
> And trust in His redeeming blood
> And try His works to do."

"We love him because he first loved us." "The heart hath reasons that the reason knows not of...!"

In the name of the Father, Son, and Holy Spirit. Amen.

General Endnotes

1   The information given about the Chicago Sunday Evening Club in the general Introduction to this section is from *www.csec.org.*

2   This sermon was presented at the Chicago Sunday Evening Club in December 1973.

3   This sermon was presented at the Chicago Sunday Evening Club in December 1974.

4   This sermon was presented at the Chicago Sunday Evening Club in December 1976.

5   This sermon was presented at the Chicago Sunday Evening Club in December 1978.

VI

Why The Beans Tasted Better

This sermon was preached as one of the Oil Patch Lectures on the Foundation established by Mr. and Mrs. Richard Claiborne at First United Methodist Church in Odessa, Texas, on February 3, 1991. The pastor was Dr. Charles Crutchfield, now a bishop. It was a wonderful experience to spend these days in that thriving city located in the midst of what appeared to me to be a nearly interminable stretch of oil well countryside. I shall never forget the warmth of these good people who remembered with such gratitude the presence on their staff of Mrs. Joe Hale, wife of the distinguished former General Secretary of the World Methodist Council.

I loved the Claibornes from the very beginning. Clarice became a member of the Board of Trustees of The Foundation for Evangelism a bit later, and, at this writing, is secretary of that board.

An interesting sidelight in my memory of this happy week is that I preached on Sunday morning (before beginning in Odessa) at Midland, Texas, a few miles away. I was told by the pastor that Mr. and Mrs. George W. Bush were seated near the front of the church during my sermon, and the pastor referred to him as the son of the President of the United States!

This particular sermon which I have titled in an extremely plebeian fashion is totally my own production, but the Scripture reference and outline were given to me by my very dear friend, the late Professor James S. Stewart of Edinburgh, Scotland.

Why The Beans Tasted Better

When I was pastor of a church in Chattanooga, Tennessee, I had a dear woman in my parish who never came to public worship. I worked on her assiduously and almost ruthlessly but with no visible effect. Until the last Sunday I stood preaching in that pulpit. I didn't know it was my last Sunday, the bishop hadn't told me. And I've always wondered how she found it out. I suppose there is such a thing as feminine clairvoyance, and if there is, she had a massive portion of it. But anyway, that Sunday she came to church, and she came all the way down to the front of the sanctuary and sat right in front of me. But she made her escape during the singing of the last hymn and I had no opportunity to greet her. About an hour later, we were seated around the table in our parsonage home having Sunday dinner. Our telephone rang—it was she. I shall never forget her words: "Preacher," she said, "I wanted you to know that the beans tasted better today because I was in church this morning."

I have read a great many books on the theory of corporate worship, but I have never heard it expressed more memorably than the way she put it. "The beans tasted better today because I was in church this morning." So, what I really want to do is speak to you just now about why the beans taste better when we go to church. But I wish to do it against the backdrop of a passage of Scripture that in all probability you have never related to church. You will find it in the 12th chapter of the Letter to the Hebrews beginning with the 22nd and continuing through the 24th verses.

> "But ye are come unto mount Sion and unto the city of the living God, the heavenly Jerusalem and to an innumerable company of angels, to the general assembly and church of the firstborn, which are written in heaven, and to God the Judge of all, and to the spirits of just men made perfect, and to Jesus the mediator of the new covenant, and to the blood of sprinkling, that speaketh better things than that of Abel."

What happens when you come to church? First of all the author of Hebrews says that when you come to church you come to a *spiritual* fellowship. "...Ye are come," says he, "unto mount Sion." The deepest of all the realities of life is the spiritual reality. We glimpse it in the eyes of a little child, we catch it in the melody of an old hymn. Curiously and unfortunately, we are living in a moment of the world's history when it is quite difficult for us to identify the spiritual. Reinhold Niebuhr, that great American theologian, shortly before he died wrote an essay in which he said, "The United States of America is a gadget-filled paradise suspended in a hell of international uncertainty." It was a perceptive observation. It isn't easy for us to think religious thoughts. Oddly enough, science is helping us to recover our consciousness of the spiritual through its insistence upon the reality of the unseen. Let me illustrate what I mean. We behold the colors of the rainbow from red on one end of the spectrum to violet on the other end of the spectrum, and we marvel at their beauty. But science comes along and tells us that beyond the red there is the infrared and beyond the violet is the ultraviolet—neither of which we can see. And beyond the infrared and the ultraviolet, there are unimaginable stretches of color, all of them utterly invisible to the physical eye.

The greatest experiences of life, the greatest content of life, can never really be measured by the means we are accustomed to employ. You cannot dole out ten gallons of courage to a United States Marine in Saudi Arabia any more than you can give a thousand kilowatts of love to an orphaned child. The greatest realities are always in the realm of the intangible, the immeasurable, the inaudible, the spiritual. And the best place in all the world to realize that is in the church. The oldest piece of furniture on earth is the altar. It was Gilbert Chesterton, that brilliant British essayist and critic, who said "The most pathetic person on this planet is the atheist who suddenly feels thankful and then remembers that he has no one to thank." A poet put it this way:

> "Our little systems have their day,
> They have their day and cease to be,
> They are but broken lights of Thee,
> And Thou, O Lord, art more than they."

When you come to church you come to a spiritual fellowship, to mount Sion.

Then the author of Hebrews goes on to say, when you come to church you come to a *universal* fellowship: "Ye are come," says he, "to the general assembly." Years ago, when I was a college president, my wife and I often went to New York City on college business. One time we happened to be there and we had an afternoon to spare before we were scheduled to return home. Neither one of us had ever seen the Cathedral of St. John the Divine. We took a taxi out to Riverside Drive and to that magnificent edifice that stands there. I remember vividly the afternoon when we made our visit. We walked into the immense nave and stood there alone gazing in the distance at the great altar, conscious of the incredibly massive and glorious architecture that rose all around us. And we looked up and saw the afternoon sun coming through the stained glass windows in slanted rays that struck the floor of the nave and helped us to see the immense room. We were so overcome by this great church that I turned to my wife and I said, "This, this is the church of the living God!" And so it was.

The next weekend we were back in the hills of Southwest Virginia, and I was keeping a promise of longstanding to one of my student pastors at Emory & Henry College and going with him to serve the sacrament of the Lord's Supper at his tiny little student church nestled away in the hills of Virginia. We rode and we rode in his ramshackle old car until at last we came to what Dr. Clovis Chappell would have called the woods behind the backwoods, and there it stood on a lovely hillside, a tiny, rustic, rural chapel built by the men who composed its membership. It was a cold December day. We went into that little sanctuary and I looked around. I saw instantly that the pulpit was handmade and the pews hand carved. There were no cushions in the pews, there was no organ or piano, just a handful of tattered old songbooks with shaped notes. In one corner of the room stood a potbellied stove, and the fire went out in that stove twice during worship. We concluded the service wearing our topcoats. But as I stood there and read the ancient ritual of Holy Communion to that little Southwest Virginia congregation composed of thirteen people, something deep down in my soul cried out again, "This, too, is the church of the living God!" Just as surely as that magnificent edifice that stands off Riverside Drive on Manhattan Island is the church of the living God, so this little rural chapel nestled in the hills of the Old Dominion is the church of the living God. The church of God is not evaluated by size but transcends geography, economics, language, culture, race and education.

> "In Christ there is no east or west,
> In Him no south or north,
> But one great fellowship of love
> Throughout the whole wide earth."

When you come to church you come to a universal fellowship,... "Ye are come to the general assembly."

Then the author of Hebrews goes on to say that when you come to church you come to an *immortal* fellowship,..."to the spirits of just men made perfect." Every once in awhile I like to stop what I am doing and remember God's giants whom I have been privileged to know in my own lifetime. I recall Edwin Holt Hughes, for so long the senior bishop of our church and

one of the architects of the 1939 unification of the three branches of American Methodism, great educator, peerless preacher who came to Chattanooga, Tennessee in the last year of his life on earth for a series of sermons during which he baptized our baby boy at the little church where I was serving. I remember Peter Marshall, that famous Scottish minister whose biography *A Man Called Peter* was written by his wife Catherine after his untimely death. I heard him half a hundred times. I still recall that muscular figure, his dark blond hair falling down over his forehead, his delightful dimples, and the delectable "brrrr" on the edge of his tongue. He was a prose poet who could reach up into the stratosphere of theological thought and bring the great truths of our holy faith down and set them to the music of his own soul. I remember George Washington Truett, who became famous for his long and distinguished pastorate at First Baptist Church in Dallas, who was born in Hayesville, North Carolina, not far from Lake Junaluska. His face looked as though it had been carved out of a piece of granite and he could pronounce the phrase "Jesus Christ" with such penetrating power that the words seared their way into your mind. I remember my own grandmother rolling out biscuit dough in the kitchen and peeling potatoes on the back porch, singing as she worked a song that isn't sung anymore:

> "I saw a wayworn traveler in tattered garments clad,
> And struggling up the mountain, it seemed that he was sad,
> His back was heavy laden, his strength was almost gone,
> Yet he shouted as he journeyed, 'Deliverance will come.'"

These were God's giants, these and ten thousand times ten thousand more who built this church across the earth and handed it to us as they went to glory. Oftentimes we have received what they did too easily, too casually, too carelessly. When you come to church you come to an immortal fellowship, to "the spirits of just men made perfect."

The best place in all the world to renew fellowship with those whom we have loved and lost awhile is in the church. I appreciate the custom of some of the European churches: they keep two rolls for every congregation, the roll of those who have been translated into that better world and the roll of those who are still part of the church militant. I believe that is the correct thing to do. But when you come to an immortal fellowship you come also to an *inextinguishable hope*. It is a haunting experience to remember the story about Marguerite Higgins, one of the great journalists of World War II. She happened to ask a Marine Sergeant on Iwo Jima one day, "If I had the power to give you anything you wanted, what would you ask for?" The Marine Sergeant, with his cigarette in his mouth, looked at her and replied with one word: "Tomorrow."

Our hearts are burdened and heavy because of our loved ones and our friends dying in faraway lands as day after day they stand for sanity and justice so that the people who live there may have the hope of freedom. We must believe that all of this is happening so that these tortured lands will have a chance for their tomorrows.

I remember years ago when I saw for the first time emblazoned over the great altar of Westminster Abbey in the city of London in golden letters the language of Revelation 11:15. For some reason it startled me when first I stood there and read: "The kingdoms of this world are become the kingdoms of our Lord and of his Christ." I wish they had completed the verse and it would have read, "...and he shall reign for ever and ever." Do you believe that? In spite of wars and rumors of wars, do you believe it? I do.

I love to read fiction, novels because you get a better portrait of human nature in them than you do sometimes in biographies and histories. But I have a bad habit for which my wife has scolded me many times across the years. I always turn over and peep at the last page. I want to see how it comes out. I want to learn whether he kisses her or not. If he doesn't kiss her, I may not even read that book. Dear friends, I want us to remember that the Christian Scriptures come out right, as in Isaiah 11:9: "The knowledge of the glory of the Lord shall cover the earth as the waters cover the sea." I am radiantly sure that this is going to happen. If I did not have this confidence, I would stop preaching. When you come to an immortal fellowship, you come also to an inextinguishable hope.

Then the author of Hebrews goes on to say that when you come to church you come to a *divine* fellowship: "...ye are come," says he, "to God and to Jesus." The church is not an earthly organization, not a Sabbath Rotary Club or a Sunday garden society. The church came down from God out of Heaven. Dr. James Moffit, when he was teaching at Drew University in this country, said to one of his classes, "We are not like a little group of lonely people kneeling down upon a tiny moor trying to prevent a spot of fire from being blown out by the great winds of the world." "The church," said Dr. Moffit, "is in far wiser hands than our hands, as indeed it always has been. What we have to do is to keep in touch with the fire; the fire will always burn." When you come to church you are not there to see what your neighbor wears, or by whose side someone is sitting. When you come to church you come to see the face of your Savior. The church is divine. Something happens in church that is not likely to happen anywhere else in all the world. And because the church is divine, you and I have a right to attempt the impossible as the children and the servants of God. When we look out at a world like ours where there is so much evil and it is so deeply entrenched and malignant, we sometimes wonder deep down in our hearts what is the use in trying to combat it? Suppose I do try to live a life for righteousness and God, what good will it do in the end? Did you ever have that thought? I have had it many times. But we forget one of the cardinal truths of the gospel. When we stand for something that is right, when we tell the truth instead of a lie, when we cast a vote in a city or a national election for someone who is on God's side, when we try to act with honor and integrity and for the good of the human cause, in a way that we can seldom understand and at a point we can rarely identify, Heaven touches our frail, fragile human effort and gives it immortal power. I believe that, too. I believe that John Henry Cardinal Newman was right when he said, "The church was formed for the express purpose of interfering with the world." I believe that. And I believe that for you and me to interfere with the world in the name of Jesus guarantees that Heaven will give meaning and effectiveness to our efforts. When you come to church, you come to a divine fellowship to God and to Jesus.

Then last of all and best of all, the author of Hebrews says that when you come to church you come to a *redemptive* fellowship. He reaches back into the Book of Exodus for his figure: "...ye are come," says he, "to the blood of sprinkling, which speaketh better things than that of Abel."

When I was serving my first church, I remember Bishop Wallace E. Brown telling a story from the early chapters of his ministry as a young preacher in New York State which I have never forgotten. One Sunday, he began to hold what my grandfather would have called a protracted meeting, or a revival, in a little country church located in the midst of a New York meadow near the banks of a great river. It was a hot July in that Empire State countryside, and not far from the little church where Wallace Brown was preaching was a tiny cottage where lived a young man and his family. This young man had committed nearly every sin a person could name. He had allowed his own life to disintegrate completely. The story of his years was a story of immorality and unfaithfulness. One afternoon he was sitting in his cottage living room when waves of remorse swept over him and he realized how he had betrayed his wife and his children and what a colossal wrongdoer he was. He decided that he would commit suicide, and without speaking to anyone he slipped out of that cottage and as the twilight closed in about him he made his way to the river bank, there to throw his body into the rushing waters. But on his way to the river bank he had to pass the little church where Wallace Brown was preaching the gospel. The windows and the doors of the church had been opened wide and he heard the people singing Fannie Crosby's old gospel song *Rescue the Perishing*. Borne on the wings of the summer air were the words of the third stanza, which we often fail to sing:

> "Down in the human heart crushed by the tempter,
> Feelings lie buried that grace can restore;
> Touched by a loving heart, wakened by kindness,
> Chords that were broken shall vibrate once more."

Something in the mysterious wonder of those words reached out and laid hold upon the tortured heart of this young man on his way to end his life. Instead of going to the river's bank, he slipped into that little country church and sat down on the back pew where in a few moments he heard Wallace Brown preach. At the close of the service the pastor gave an invitation for those who wanted to have their sins forgiven and their lives remade, and this prodigal young husband and father, grasping for a hope he had not known about until then, went down the center aisle and fairly threw himself at the chancel railing. Again, as my grandfather would have said, with the pastor's guidance he prayed through. At the close of the service they had another circle of prayer, and then, arm-in-arm, the pastor and Wallace Brown walked with this young man, who had found God at that little rural altar, across the countryside until they came to the little cottage which he had departed in despair an hour or so before. There, joined by the young man's family, they had a reunion of love, forgiveness and hope. The years flew by, and Wallace Brown became a bishop of The Methodist Church. He had spoken one evening in a midwestern city and there awaited him at the close of the service a handsome middle-aged man. Wallace Brown greeted him and the following exchange of conversation took place: "You don't remember me, do you, Bishop Brown?" Wallace Brown acknowledged that he did not remember him and the man smiled as he asked, "Do you remember the night long ago when you preached in a little church in New York State on a hot July evening, and a man on his way to commit suicide stopped in the church, heard you preach, and found God that evening?" "I shall never forget that night on earth or in Heaven," replied Bishop Brown. "Of course I remember." The man looked into the bishop's eyes and said, "I am that person, and I wanted you to know that the experience I had years ago is still as real and vivid to me now as it was when it happened. What have you been doing with yourself since then, Bishop Brown?" Wallace Brown looked at him and said, "I've been trying to go up and down the earth saying a good word for Jesus Christ." "Oh," said his friend, "you must keep doing that, but, Bishop Brown, as you go up and down the earth, don't forget to say a good word for the church of Jesus Christ, too, for if that church hadn't been in that New York meadow years and years ago, my body would have lain on the river's bottom before midnight." When you come to church you come to a redemptive fellowship: you come to a land of beginning again no matter what you have done, no matter the mistakes you have made, no matter the sins you have committed. You come to the place where you can cast aside the dark memories of the past and where God in the wonder of his grace will allow you to begin life afresh, life in the resurrection power of God's Risen Son.

This is the business of the church. You come to a spiritual fellowship, a universal fellowship, an immortal fellowship and an indistinguishable hope, a divine fellowship and a redemptive fellowship. No wonder the beans tasted better! The greatest thing that can ever happen to a human being on this earth is for that person to enter into a personal relationship with the Lord Jesus Christ and to become a part for a little while of the church which is His body.

A while back my wife and I were in Washington, DC and one evening we went to the Kennedy Center for the Performing Arts and listened to the National Symphony Orchestra play Gustav Mahler's little-known Second Symphony, the "Resurrection Symphony." I think I have never heard such magnificent music. The triumphant message of the Risen Christ broke through the stirring measures of the symphony with surpassing power. It was an overwhelming experience, and I have thought of it many, many times since. So it is that, for the Christian at worship, the gloom and despair of life's burdens and troubles are suddenly shattered by the crashing chords of the Resurrection truth and promise. The darkness of the night is flooded with unearthly light. Our faith and our hope are secure in the Risen Redeemer. This is the message communicated through the fellowships which compose the church. Some may find this blessing of blessings in other places, but it is in His church, praise God, that this transforming miracle is most likely to occur!

VII

The Ruminations of An Ex-President

This address was delivered on Charter Day, March 20, 1985, at Emory & Henry College upon the deeply appreciated invitation of Dr. Charles Sydnor, 18th president of this institution and my former student. Charles has had an unusually successful career in which his college presidency holds a prominent place. All of the chief executives of this "little Oxford in the wilderness" who have followed me have made unquestionably noteworthy achievements. William C. Finch, Glenn Mingledorf, Thomas F. Chilcote, Jr., Charles Sydnor and (at the present) Thomas R. Morris have worn the presidential medallion since 1964. I could comment on each of them, including reference to my long and pleasant personal friendship with Tom Chilcote, but I select two who deserve very special mention. Bill Finch, who succeeded me, is, I think, undoubtedly the finest academician we have had in the college's modern history. He was already nationally known when he came to us, and he left unusual marks of excellence at Emory & Henry. The other name that I offer is that of Tom Morris, who has done so very much to build the endowment and to augment the physical structures of this institution and whose brilliant scholarship is recognized across the Old Dominion.

My days of visiting Emory & Henry College are over, but my storehouse of recollections of my own eight supremely happy years there is rich both in quantity and in quality.

The Ruminations of An Ex-President

President Sydnor, Bishop Eutsler, members of the faculty, members of the Board of Trustees, distinguished representatives from other institutions and societies, ladies and gentlemen: This, in a very particular way, is a day that belongs to the Sydnors. It is for my wife and myself a unique and memorable privilege to share this day with them. They finished Emory & Henry as students just after we had departed, but we knew them across most of the years of their student generation, and we recognized then their unusual leadership capacities and potential. The years flew by. Charles Sydnor walked the long educational road to a specialization in German and European History, to rôles as classroom teacher, college administrator, writer and producer of educational television, man of affairs in the life of a great state, and as a constantly more significant citizen, not only of his Commonwealth, but of our nation and world. And so my first and most pleasant privilege is to salute the eighteenth president of Emory & Henry College, Dr. Charles Sydnor, and to wish for him and his lovely wife years of happiness and a sense of achievement, fulfillment and historic accomplishment here on the campus which now belongs to them twice.

In one of his long poems entitled "Build Soil," Robert Frost had these lines:

> "Don't join too many groups, join few if any;
> Join the United States and join the family,
> But not much in between unless a college."

What is there about a college that intertwines its character and personality with the strings of our hearts? This is for me, as you would know, a time of nostalgia, of happy and grateful remembrance. When I was President of Emory & Henry College, I heard a great deal about students' rights. In an old catalog of this institution, published in the 19th century, there is this sentence: "Students have few if any rights of their own and all of these may be taken away from them at the will of the administration." Now, to be sure, we know that this is not true. I doubt if it was ever true, even in those faraway days when that sentence was composed. I have been pondering my own memories of eight happy years of identification with institutional Christian higher education, pondering them in the light of my later thinking and, for that matter, later learning. I have persuaded myself that students do indeed have certain *inalienable rights*, particularly in an institution like Emory & Henry College, which rights can never be taken away from them by an administrator or anyone.

First, I am persuaded that a student at such a college has *the right to experience a different kind of education*—an education with academic substance. There is occurring throughout the educational scene today a series of events and developments which, in my judgment, threatens the *quality* of higher education in a way that is, to put it mildly, perilous. The National Institute of Education revealed to us recently that graduate record examinations showed a decline in eleven of fifteen subject areas between 1964 and 1982. We are further informed that the number of arts and science degrees granted in qualified American institutions has dropped thirteen percent in the last eleven years. Academic substance is at the root of the educational experience. The church needs to realize that its colleges are not extended Sunday Schools and the educational world needs to insist upon the recovery of the kind of academic muscle which can arm the young men and the young women of a new generation for the stupendous new tasks now confronting this national and western civilization.

This different kind of education means also a college which still teaches the student how to think, how to evaluate, how to examine critically. The current kind of education which has become basically utilitarian in the life of this Republic, it seems to me, has departed dangerously from that fundamental function.

Furthermore, this different kind of education calls for a college which communicates culture, teaches significant graces, and insists upon courtesy, consideration for others and the use of proper amenities in interpersonal contacts. If you will permit a nearly ridiculous digression at this point, I have noticed multiple instances in ordinary and even fine restaurants of the inexcusable practice of well-dressed American men wearing their headgear throughout entire meals. I confess that I have been tempted to step over to such a person and actually lift off his hat and hand it to him—a deed which would likely produce its own retaliatory action against me! What I am trying to say is that unless we can recover some of those cultural graces that in other days have set apart the educated, the civilized woman or man from others, we shall have failed at least partially in the educational attempt.

Moreover, this different kind of education expected of an institution like Emory & Henry calls for a college which still believes in the Christian witness, but not a college which thrusts religion down the throats of students. If I were a college president today, I would not attempt to do that as much as perhaps I did when I was one, for I am convinced that such is not only bad religion and bad psychology, but also bad manners. Nor do I believe that you can build a Christian institution of higher learning simply by enforcing a rule against drinking or, for that matter, against anything that is substantively classified as a violation of religious morality. I believe the only way to build a Christian college is to assemble a Christian faculty. In most instances, with the exception of specific courses in the field, their business is not to teach religion *per se*, but only by indirection as the orientation of the teacher's life becomes a setting for instruction. I do not believe that a college like Emory & Henry can long survive apart from its insistence upon the Christian witness.

Second, I am convinced that the student in this kind of college has an *inalienable right* to *have it all fall apart* on him or her at least once. We forget that education includes the privilege of failure, the right to doubt, permission to become all mixed up! When I was president here, I had to suspend two young men. I told myself at the time that they were not essentially bad people. In due time, they enrolled in other institutions, graduated from those institutions, and I began to receive a Christmas card from each of them, always with a Bible verse appropriately chosen and penned. One Christmas I got a card from one of them notifying me that he had been ordained a minister in The United Methodist Church. You know there was something embarrassing if not downright humiliating in that. But, Charles, I learned something while I was here: never give up on a student, for the chances are you will give up on the wrong one! And somewhere down the way, he or she will start sending you Christmas cards with Scripture quotations. The student has an inalienable right to have it all fall apart at least once; this is part of the educational experience!

Third, another inalienable right of students in this kind of a college is that of having his or her *mind stretched, enlarged, changed*. Robert Frost said the purpose of education is to help us get over our little-mindedness. There is truth in that. For you know, we are provincial, parochial, but being so is not an accident of geography. It is a state of mind. The horizons of the heart, the frontiers of the intellect have vanished. Today our world is confronted by a galaxy of new problems: an overpopulated earth, a pluralistic culture, the phenomenon of the third world, and that incredible invader of industry, government, education, commerce and even life itself, *the computer*—to mention but a few. Somehow the mind and spirit of the student educated in these halls here must be enlarged to encompass not only these problems, but also their management and solutions. When I was at Emory & Henry, I used to say there were at least four builders of the new South, men who had become bold architects of a fresh day in this part of our nation: Ralph McGill, the great Atlanta editor; Benjamin Mays, that incredible pioneer in education and race relations who left us just a few months ago; Frank Porter Graham (who at one time gave a commencement address at this institution), former president of the consolidated Universities of North Carolina, Senator from North Carolina and United Nations staff member; and Willis D. Weatherford, that brilliant sociologist of the South, local Elder in The Methodist Church whose son became president of

Berea College. These four men were all courageous beyond their time, prophetic in their viewpoints, sensitive, compassionate. What Emory & Henry College needs to do, dear friends, is to turn men and women like them loose in society, to make again a new and a better South, a nation dedicated to unselfish international citizenship, and a world safe for freedom and justice in the most dangerous hour of human history ever known. The right to have his or her mind stretched, enlarged, changed is a student's inalienable right in a college like Emory & Henry.

Fourth, there is the right to prepare *to confront the wrongs of the world*. When that diminutive little preacher from Florida, J. Wallace Hamilton, spoke years ago at Emory University during the turbulence of the 1960s, the student body was angry. He looked out at his resentful young audience and said, "If you see things that don't suit you in your world, why don't you go out and raise hell about them?" Dare I say to you that one of the indispensable ingredients of an authentic educational experience is learning *how to raise constructive hell*? When I was here as president, we had the beginnings of the violent anger of the 1960s. No president who ever lived through a portion of that time or all of it can ever forget it. Now we have the self-centered inertia of the 1980s; and if you ask me, I would rather deal with anger than inertia! There is no way to get hold of the latter. Did you ever try to tie a knot in chocolate pudding? Somehow we have to attempt to build a fire under students today so that their concerns will go beyond getting a job or earning a decent salary or the achievement of earthly comfort, luxury and happiness. The ills of the world are such that only an informed, awakened and committed student mind and heart can address them in time to save the world for our children and grandchildren. Reading the story of our country has always been one of my choice avocations. I have discovered that it is the broadly educated and deeply concerned characters in the annals of United States history who have dared to venture into the realm of new ideas which later became the building blocks of our American civilization. People like Thomas Jefferson, author of the Declaration of Independence and founder of the University of Virginia, James Madison, a leading figure in composing the Constitution, and Woodrow Wilson, president of Princeton University and later chief executive of our nation during the first World War, were all leaders who combined a vast knowledge with daring initiative. I stood outside Mr. Wilson's postwar home on S Street in Washington and remembered how he struggled to obtain the approval of his country for the utterly new concept of the League of Nations near the close of the Peace Conference. His efforts were not successful, and Premier Georges Clemenciau of France remarked somewhat caustically, "The United States is not ready to have a President whose father was a Presbyterian minister!" But the miracle came later: the League of Nations became the parent idea for the United Nations! It is not an exaggerated contemplation when we express the hope that the students of this college and others like it will find themselves able to propose something new for the good of the human family—and they can do this without becoming chief executives of our country! They would be patriots of the first order, for it is a major blunder to equate patriotism with the *status quo*.

Fifth, a student in an institution like this has an *inalienable right to grow into the kind of young man or woman with whom he or she can live*. The educational process is curious. When you graduate, there are so many facts you never remember, but there will always be a few things which you will recall. You remember your friends, and a book or two you read, maybe on no professor's reading list. You remember a few immense personalities, not many, just a few—and if a college ever reaches a point where it does not have immense personalities, its educational coefficient is alarmingly reduced. You recall the impact a certain course had on your life when suddenly you felt the chains falling away and you were free. You remember a person you knew who was better than you were and who bothered you just because of that fact. You can never forget a thing you did that was wrong and nobody ever found out about it. You recall one or two great addresses you heard, a kindness somebody did for you, someone you loved or thought you did, and a wonderful moment when God or something very like Him broke into your life. All of this is an educational experience. Oh, the facts are necessary, the logic is important, but quite beyond all of that, these are the things that help a young man or a young woman to grow into the kind of person with whom he or she can live.

Then *last of all*, there is the *inalienable right* of a student at a college like Emory & Henry to *believe in the future*. That requires *honesty*. You may remember that John Gardner said, "We know the values to which we are being unfaithful. This patient's disease is not confusion, it's infidelity." It also requires *courage*. It was last autumn that the students at Brown University petitioned the administration to stockpile cyanide pills so that if the hour of nuclear disaster appeared about to come while they were there, there would be an easier way out than the agony accompanying the final holocaust. A citizen of Paris in the days of the French Revolution was asked what he did. He said, "I survived." But there must be more than that. There has to be *hope*. Honesty, courage and hope. Remember Genesis 18:25, Abraham's question: "Shall not the judge of all the earth do right?" Also recall in the Book of Judges, the 5th chapter and the 20th verse: "The stars in their courses fought against Sisera." What does that mean? It means simply that there is at the heart of creation as we know it an integrity, a commitment to justice and righteousness upon which a student in today's crazy mixed-up world may yet depend. It means that the unannounced part of the curriculum of any institution of higher learning dedicated to Jesus Christ must be a belief in the future.

I was at the Smithsonian Institution in Washington not too long ago, wandering among the exhibits, and I came to the reconstruction of a chemical laboratory presided over by a man named Robert E. Humphreys. It was in this chemical laboratory many, many years ago that Robert Humphreys discovered the thermal process for cracking petroleum to produce gasoline. He took that discovery to John D. Rockefeller and sold it, and so the dawn of the motor age with all of its vast, illimitable implications came. On the little Smithsonian plaque that described this experimentation, there was the simple announcement that Robert Humphreys was a graduate of Emory & Henry College, Class of 1889. It was Dr. Humphreys who gave the organ in Memorial Chapel here in memory of his wife during the last years of his life. And as I stood there and read again that plaque and gazed upon that apparatus, I remember how Mr. Culberson and I visited him in a suburb of Chicago when he was past ninety. An inspiring recollection that speaks thrillingly of what this college has done for this Republic, but, dear friends, what a member of the Class of 1889 did won't amount to a hill of beans in structuring a viable future for Emory & Henry College in days ahead. It is what you and I do *now*, and what happens under the administration of President Sydnor that will determine the tomorrows of this institution.

May God grant that there will be sufficient reason for the careers of graduates of this institution to be commemorated not only in the Smithsonian Institution, but in the National Archives and wherever history is written during the long years that lie ahead. God bless and keep our new president, his family, his administration, and God prosper Emory & Henry College! *Macte virtute*!!

VIII

Pen Portraits

I have selected five individuals who have figured prominently in the unfolding of the Christian mission in the last half of the twentieth century. Three of these are bishops, one is an authentically great educator and the fourth is an ecclesiastical reformer who left a precious legacy to his church.

It would be quite impossible to overstate the wide variety represented by these choices, and I must confess that this has been deliberate on my part. The panel is eclectic—as is the church itself.

I have borrowed the term "pen portraits" from the late Bishop Roy H. Short. The stylistic features of these writings are neither uniform nor consistent, because they originated in widely different settings.

James Kenneth Mathews

Bishop Mathews is a gloriously unique United Methodist leader, and when his era is over it is doubtful if future Christians will see any true reproduction of his remarkable gifts and graces.

It should be noted that he was elected a bishop first in India, but declined to accept the office there because of his conviction that it should be filled by a native son or daughter. His subsequent election in the United States was accomplished in his absence from that particular Jurisdictional Conference. Surely these facts compose an imposing but intangible credential for this high office.

He is now well along in his tenth decade and retains an authoritative voice in the Council of Bishops. The following pen portrait of him (and his wife Eunice) appeared as the Introduction to his autobiography Global Odyssey and is used here with the permission of the publisher and also with the consent of Bishop Mathews.

James Kenneth Mathews

More than a century ago, in Boston's old Trinity Church, Phillips Brooks reminded us that "Every true life has its Jerusalem to which it is always going up." These words suggest the ultimate role of a compelling and controlling purpose in structuring the real meaning of an individual's earthly pilgrimage. Fortunate indeed is the man or woman who achieves this focus in his or her career, particularly if the stimulus for such motivation has a Divine origin. Bishop Mathews' remarkable autobiography entitled *Global Odyssey* chronicles the life of one who has made and is making the long journey to his Jerusalem with happy abandon and sacred commitment.

James Kenneth Mathews, as his colleagues in the Council of Bishops and many others in the United Methodist and ecumenical worlds see it, has brought both effectiveness and honor to God's church through his adventurous and distinguished life.

Referring again to *Global Odyssey*, there is something almost massive about this venture in autobiography—its immense sweep, its rich detail, its cast of characters both famous and obscure, its frequent unstudied stylistic elegance, and its vast array of topics. The bishop reviews his long career with candor and without the disenchanting guise of false modesty. He writes with no sense of *denouement* and makes it quite clear that he has never believed in retirement for a Christian minister.

Sitting near Bishop Mathews in a meeting of the Council of Bishops, as I have done upon many occasions, provokes both reflection and appreciation. He presents an impressive image of buoyant health and easy, undiminished vigor. His native dignity befits his office and equips him to move gracefully among both the elite and the ordinary in any setting. There is about him a gentle and pleasant austerity that never quite abridges the gracious warmth of genuine cordiality. He follows the agenda closely, as he did before his several retirements, and courteously ignores points of trivia in discussions, quickly identifying major issues and, with fair frequency, interjecting illuminating and insightful comments that often guide the Council's thought toward wiser conclusions. That he is in the latter half of his ninth decade rarely occurs to his colleagues and perhaps never to him. He remains, after four retirements, an episcopal figure of strong and constructive influence.

Let me suggest a very important point which needs to be made in any adequate assessment of Bishop Mathews' life. One can never evaluate the varied and substantial accomplishments of Jim Mathews in either the missionary or the episcopal eras of his life without acknowledging the far more than usual role played in it all by his brilliant and extraordinary wife, Eunice Jones Mathews, the only child of Dr. and Mrs. E. Stanley Jones, perhaps Methodism's premier missionary couple of the twentieth century. Born in India, she met Jim during his early days as a missionary pastor in what was then the city of Bombay. To catalog the multiple gifts and accomplishments of this proudly independent and charming lady would be a major challenge. It is enough to say that the lovely threads of Eunice's own creative life are interwoven with those of her husband's to compose a rich tapestry of thoughtful meaning in modern Kingdom history.

Bishop Mathews' career has earned him a cluster of ecclesiastical appellations: missionary, evangelist (the two he prefers), social activist, ecumenist, scholar, author, preacher, teacher, and bishop. In all of his roles he has exemplified a rare and remarkable balance between personal and social religion. His intimate and treasured knowledge of Jesus Christ as his personal Savior and Lord reflects the best of the ancient orthodoxy whose theology glorified the New Testament church. Yet his keenly sensitive social conscience has made him acutely aware of every human deviation from Divinely designed standards of right and wrong in earthly relationships. His effort to stand vigorously and with intelligence and courage for Heaven's norms has been lifelong and uncompromising. Both the personal and social poles of the Christian religion have been safely ensconced within the shelter of his broad and vibrant evangelical faith. Unfortunately this has not always been an accurate description of Christian leadership. It may well be that the church's historical failure to equate its profession of faith with its passion for social action, and vice versa, is the most reasonable explanation for the gospel's long deferred total victory through the so-called Christian centuries. We have had our splendid periods of creedal emphasis and equally our splendid eras of social activism—but we have never seemed able to combine the two in adequate balance at any one time.

Possibly excepting the instance of the bishop's famous father-in-law, I have not seen, during my years, as satisfying and inspiring an example of this kind of theological balance in a Christian leader of recognized distinction as that embodied in the life and work of James K. Mathews. He is at once a devout personal evangelical (to use this word properly and in its classic sense) and an articulate social activist.

The range of Bishop Mathews' knowledge is startling. It reaches deeply into the realms of religious, cultural, historical, political and sociological scholarship. He and his wife are understandably influenced by the vivid lore of two vastly dissimilar traditions: India in the East and America in the West, both enormously important cultures on this planet. It may not be a verbal extravagance to suggest that Bishop Mathews approaches being a true Renaissance man as much or more than any modern person who has carried the bishop's staff in our church.

Perhaps because of my wife's and my own long-time appreciation for Jim and Eunice Mathews, and the fact that we view with awe the incredible accumulation of their involvements and achievements, I have set these paragraphs in what may appear to be a context of rather consistent seriousness. This is not a complete picture. Friends of the Mathews are aware that the bishop and his spouse are pleasant, charming companions for any occasion, intimately familiar with laughter and light-hearted conversation. Their hospitality, always warm and comfortable, nevertheless has an unmistakable touch of elegance about it. This does not mean, however, that it cannot become, when appropriate, quite gala. As an example, some of us recall an impromptu festivity at the close of a recent Council of Bishops evening session when Jim surprised the entire Council and its guests with a lavish, multi-flavored ice cream party to honor Eunice on her birthday!

Bishop Mathews makes it very clear that he elects to think of himself as a missionary and evangelist, choosing these designations even above that of bishop (which in no way diminishes in anybody's mind the splendid episcopal leadership he has given). The typical Christian missionary (who is always in the best sense an evangelist as well) exemplifies a unique and extraordinary excellence among those who undertake vocational service to the church. The basic selflessness of the "missionary mind" across the centuries has proved to be a major factor in conserving the motivational purity of the Christian ministry. Both Jim and Eunice Mathews have provided significant documentation for these observations. His has been a life of authentic eminence and telling impact in the history of twentieth century Christianity.

The Mathews perspective, when honestly examined, reveals a very evident and stimulating flavor of a forward look, the exciting hint of future tasks and better things to come. Jim Mathews, in his writing and his speaking, tells about the yesterdays but still lives deliberately in the tomorrows. He is, indeed, a "pilgrim of the future," to borrow Pierre Teilhard de Chardin's fascinating self-description.

Once, years ago, I heard Bishop Mathews' distinguished brother Dr. Joseph Mathews address an episcopal audience and refer to his listeners as "princes of the church." Not many of us have deserved that lofty title. In my opinion, James Kenneth Mathews does.

Robert Fielden Lundy

This piece, written in March 2005, celebrates the life and memory of a close and lifelong friend.

Very few individuals in the annals of the modern church possessed the dramatic power to impress that was the peculiar gift of Bishop Lundy. I would have to say that I seriously doubt that there has been another Methodist leader who had an opportunity to continue his or her career in the episcopacy and deliberately created legislation that made such impossible.

He and his wife were staunch friends of Mary Ann and myself—and they still are!

Robert Fielden Lundy

Robert Fielden Lundy was an unforgettable human being. The son of a distinguished father and a mother who slipped into immortality during his adolescence, he came quite early to his own keenly personal dedication to Jesus Christ and His ministry. His initial commitment underwent steady deepening across a busy lifetime of more than fourscore years.

He was graduated *cum laude* from Emory & Henry College, which institution honored him with the degree of doctor of divinity in 1961. He completed his master of divinity work at Emory University and became a student of Far East languages at Yale University for two additional years of intense study. His remarkable mastery of the very difficult Mandarin Chinese language was widely known and acknowledged throughout his lifetime.

Dr. Lundy initially had a very significant ministry in this country, organizing and nurturing into early strength what is now the great First United Methodist Church in Oak Ridge, Tennessee. From his student days, he had an extremely inquisitive mind and combined an extraordinary balance and comprehensive view of the Christian Gospel and Mission with a refreshingly different but highly developed skill in articulating it. The strong sinews of his spoken and written English had about them a plain but vigorous beauty. This unusual quality in the work of a young minister left an indelible mark upon First Church in Oak Ridge.

In 1950 Robert and Elizabeth (Hall) Lundy began their memorable service as missionaries of our church in Southeast Asia. They brought to this involved assignment unusual skill, understanding and a necessary quiet patience. Their work was varied, including pastorates of large churches in Kuala Lumper, Ipoh and Singapore, the editorship of Southeast Asia's denominational organ, *The Methodist Message*, two turns as District Superintendent, president of the Council of Christian Churches of Malaya, and finally in 1964 election as Bishop of the Southeast Asia Central Conference and the 361st bishop listed in the historical record in the *Book of Discipline*.

Bishop Lundy served his Central Conference well and participated actively in the affairs of the Council of Bishops during the quadrennium 1964–68. He served under a term episcopacy. His astute knowledge of our church in Southeast Asia and his constant readiness to place the welfare of the Christian cause ahead of any personal aspiration led him to propose legislation which made it mandatory for that Central Conference to elect a native son or daughter as bishop, thus ruling out any possibility for his own service in that high office beyond a single quadrennium.

In 1968 the Lundys concluded eighteen years of dangerously creative service in a part of the world where freedom and independence were struggling to be born, and returned to the United States for service in New York City, Atlanta, and finally in Holston, their home conference, where he was senior pastor of a great church and District Superintendent. When retirement came, he had completed officially a career as a heroic servant of God on two continents. However, his years of alleged retirement were wonderfully full of vigorous activity in the world of missions and his local church.

It is hard to capture in mere words that certain something which set Bob Lundy apart from so many of his peers and made his life a beautiful phenomenon in modern Christian history. I have the stirring recollection of the choir of Long's Chapel United Methodist Church in procession down a central aisle on Sunday morning with Bishop Lundy walking as one of them, his imposing figure progressing in quiet but stately dignity until he reached his place in the choir loft. In spite of his uniquely brilliant intellect and his capacity for incisive thought, his person was constantly clothed in a self-effacing humility, so much a part of his nature that he was likely quite unaware of it. He was a genuinely modest individual whose influence came with silent power and not as a result of overt effort.

Robert Lundy had the rare ability to present his thoughts in the garments of memorable eloquence. He was at home with great ideas, but when he was overcome with the power of one of them, he seemed simply to go apart and live with it for awhile until he was able to communicate it in appropriately vivid language. He was an incurable romanticist, and his mind regularly soared into the stratosphere of visions, although he could be as practical as potatoes.

With all of his familiarity with the work-a-day world and its mundane problems, Bishop Lundy made out of his knowledge of the great doctrines of the church a rich repertoire of classical evangelical truth. He preached an old-fashioned religion replete with the concepts of repentance, forgiveness, the efficacy of prayer and the assurance of Life Eternal. The last became especially important to him in the final months and years of his life. His remarkable mind saw to it that both the products of his pen and his proclamations from the pulpit had in them a predictable magnificence of content.

Bishop Lundy's family life was exemplary. His love for his wife was delightfully visible, and his pride in their children became significantly evident in the elements of parental guidance with which he surrounded them. For one like myself who knew the bishop from university days until his Homegoing, there was always a curious mixture of a charmingly fun-loving person and a startlingly probing intellect whose findings were filled with challenge.

Good night, dearest of friends, citizen of two worlds, God's dreamer... morning will soon come!

F. Thomas Trotter

The quadrennium 1980–1984 was a period when I was privileged to work constantly and intimately with Dr. F. Thomas Trotter, General Secretary of The Board of Christian Higher Education and Ministry. My four-year term of office as president of this Board placed me in this position.

Dr. Trotter, as I attempted to show in the address which follows, was a refreshingly creative bureaucrat who not only discharged the business of an erudite company of Board members, but also with delightful frequency sought and found ways to draw forth from them new and sometimes nearly revolutionary contributions. This particular address, given at the Claremont School of Theology in Claremont, California, on September 20, 1997, does not describe adequately his presidency of Alaska Pacific University. In this role he left a record of which the University, the church and all of his friends were justly proud. Since the address was given, he served as acting president of the Claremont School of Theology while a search was made for the school's permanent chief executive.

Dr. Trotter is a rare and wonderful human being, possessed of a quiet and sometimes irresistible charm of which he is beautifully unaware.

F. Thomas Trotter

Mr. Chairman and Friends:

Good evening, Brother Tom! As far as I know you have never asked for anything for yourself, and the gratitude you may be feeling for this evening set aside to recognize Gania and you is very likely accompanied by a measure of misery because you have to endure it! But try to relax. You had it coming to you! And, Gania, what I am about to say concerning your husband is intended for you as well, for you have been his indispensable accomplice in all of it.

Dr. Ernest Cadman Colwell, sometime President of the University of Chicago and the first President of Claremont School of Theology, son of a Methodist parsonage, New Testament scholar and a layperson, "Pomp" as we often called him, once made one of the most profound statements about the church that I ever heard: "If I must choose between keeping the Church and letting the University go, and keeping the University and letting the Church go, I will keep the Church and let the University go, for the Church would have the intelligence to build the University again." So, in our tradition, the church and the University, the altar and the study desk, the spirit and the intellect have always been viewed as belonging together. Dr. F. Thomas Trotter is as good an illustration of this sacred marriage as we have had in my lifetime.

To recall the primacy of loving God with one's mind, it seems to me, has peculiar relevance at this moment for American Christians. The current nature of so much of organized religion, particularly the growing megachurch movement, and the sad plight of modern homiletics, often appear to discourage intentional intellectual depth and the kind of rich personal faith it can produce. So, the celebration of this historic Wesleyan perspective, as it is represented so well in the person we honor tonight, may have a special appropriateness.

Time, for the Christian, can only find its proper meaning when it is understood within the context of eternity. I have come to feel, in my more mature years, that liberal religion's two greatest losses in our day may have been an awareness of the supernatural and a sense of eternity. It is true that we severely abused and misinterpreted both before we abandoned them, but it would have been far better to correct our misconceptions than to destroy our principles. Religion, at its best, always involves the reality of another world; and when a horizontal humanism seeks to eliminate this factor, the very soul of faith is threatened. I have long suspected that the life and work of Dr. Trotter reflect a perceptive consciousness of this enormous peril.

I find it nearly impossible to conceive of Tom Trotter's thought apart from his extraordinary and sensitive use of the idea of "wonder." He has spoken about it in many places for many years. I first read, now long ago, a brief piece from his pen entitled "The Flattening of Wonder" which turned out to be a sobering analysis of how the prosaic, mundane, earthy intellectual acrobatics of our contemporary culture have spilled over into the modern church's theology and worship. For a lifetime he has talked about "transcendence" and how our task has always been to capture and mediate it in and through earthen vessels. When we worked together, I saw on many occasions solid evidences of his deft administrative skills, but I constantly sensed as well a spiritual loftiness and a gentle mysticism in much of what he did.

Mae Sarton, that fascinating, sometimes inscrutable Vermont poet and novelist who remained my good friend from the days of my college presidency until her death, often told her student audiences that, if they aspired to literary careers, it would be necessary for them to see to it that "enough epiphanies happened to them." Tom Trotter, both as minister and educator, has spent a lifetime encouraging a sufficient number of epiphanies to occur all around him.

For Tom Trotter the grandeur of Aristotle's premise that all philosophy begins with a sense of wonder is extended to account for our attitudes toward the Christian religion, and particularly our approach to worship and our development of an eschatological hope. But it also translates for him as an educator into the moral quality of higher learning, and thence into the nitty-gritty of adapting academic tools and processes to become useful servants of such a lofty objective. I do not know of any other leader in our time who has both proposed and comprehended a more exciting or defensible rationale for the existence of the Christian college and university.

Anyone who has known and worked with Tom must be aware of his nearly encyclopedic knowledge of the arts—painting, sculpture, architecture, music, drama and literature—and of the beautifully articulate way in which he has woven all of this into the fabric of his ministry. He has always known what religious art is, but—more than this—the wholeness of his artistic mind and heart has informed his theological understanding and spoken through all that he has done —his teaching, his preaching, his administration—and so has created a rich and intriguing framework for all his many accomplishments.

What a career Dr. Trotter has had! Seminary professor and dean, general secretary of a great Board, university president, scholar, academic and bureaucratic innovator, and Christian minister plenipotentiary to the mind of United Methodism. . . . We can note only a few items in the precious legacy he has given to us:

- Architect of the first Doctor of Ministry program
- Pioneer in the accreditation of theological seminaries
- Leader in providing church-based legal consultation services for colleges and universities
- Creator of important publications, including: *Lex Collegii, Quarterly Review, Occasional Papers,* and *Colleague*
- Leader in the development of the United Methodist Foundation for Christian Higher Education, and author of its effort to build a $100 million scholarship fund for United Methodist college students ($35 million is already committed)
- A primary founder of Africa University
- Organizer in 1975 of the National Commission on United Methodist Higher Education which produced five volumes whose findings have shaped the work of the General Board of Higher Education and Ministry for more than two decades, and have impacted far wider ecclesiastical and academic communities as well

But the exciting sum of his deeds and their influence can never be captured in a brief review or even a more extensive catalogue. One catches a glimpse of the whole by reading some of his sermons and essays (too few of which are in print. Bob Conn's book of selections is priceless). The entire impact of his ministry is far, far greater than the words used tonight to describe it.

He is not perfect—except perhaps when he is reciting baseball statistics! Certainly not on the tennis court or (more recently) the golf course. He has developed certain delectable eccentricities that compassion compels me not to detail. He is ruthlessly color-blind and relentlessly anti-sexist. He is innocently guilty of a gentle naiveté that has crippled permanently his political correctness. He is courteously tolerant of others with totally different perspectives. Yet he has never really deviated from a steady course toward his own life goals, driven by deep personal convictions and a quiet moral urgency. He has always kept inviolate his sense of wistful wonder, and the story of his remarkable career with its vast philosophical and literary resources and its informed and balanced biblical and theological erudition cannot be told without an awesome feeling that, in his life and work, another world has impinged upon this one.

Somewhere Tom has used a lovely sentence from the writings of Joseph Conrad. Conrad described the role of the artist in civilization as that of providing for tired, distracted, bemused people "that glimpse of truth for which they have forgotten to ask." This seems to summarize much of what Tom Trotter has been doing in the classroom, the administrative office, the pulpit and the world. We may not see his like again.

I am confident, Brother Tom, that I have made you sufficiently uncomfortable tonight. But, as I said in the beginning, you had it coming to you! So often it happens that the church does not elect its greatest daughters and sons to the episcopacy, and you are additional and eloquent evidence of this fact. We love you and honor you, and thank God for you and Gania!

William Ragsdale Cannon, Jr.

The Good Lord made only one William Ragsdale Cannon, Jr., and then He broke the mold!

Bill Cannon was indescribably unique and dangerously intelligent. His remarkable academic record is exceedingly rare in the annals of American education. His encyclopedic memory startled anyone who encountered it. He was completely at home with the most profound thoughts produced by the human mind across the centuries. And yet he maintained until his death in the ninth decade of his life a classical childlikeness that would evidence itself at the most unexpected times and cause the person with whom he was talking to deal suddenly with an idea or a concept whose appearance, if this person had not known Bishop Cannon previously, came as a staggering surprise. He was happily unmarried across his lifetime and many of his conversations had a naiveté about them which even those of us who knew him best could never be quite sure was genuine: his oral visitations, we realized, were often deliberately contrived to cause us to reveal additional facts he knew we had.

In spite of these delicious eccentricities, Bill Cannon brought to the episcopacy a richness of its traditional lore which we have not quite encountered anywhere else in United Methodism.

I loved him.

William Ragsdale Cannon, Jr.[1]

I first met William Ragsdale Cannon, Jr. when he became a member of the faculty of the Candler School of Theology at Emory University in 1943 while I was a student there. His remarkable academic accomplishments at the University of Georgia and Yale at first impressed some of us less than his proclivity for giving his students low grades. We began to avoid his classes so conspicuously that President Goodrich White (so the rumor went) had to have a heart-to-heart talk with the young professor about the rarity of encountering his own level of intellectual astuteness in the average student mind. After this the low marks ceased or at least diminished, and across the long future years the pendulum of the Cannon perspective appeared to swing to the opposite extreme as he again and again lavished huge amounts of extravagant praise upon many of us whose ordinariness could never justify such adulation.

Our friendship deepened during the period from 1945–1950, and broadened to include my wife, our baby son and my parents who lived with us as we served a fledgling church that worshiped in a seventy-five year old farmhouse in Chattanooga, Tennessee. Bill often preached for me there, driving up from his native Dalton, Georgia, and sometimes bringing his Mother along. I have three delightful memories of those days: his holding his Bible against his heart and then quoting unerringly from memory the long, often obscure passage of Scripture from which he was going to preach; his casual practice, as he preached, of swatting flies that had come through the open windows of our improvised edifice on a hot July Sunday morning, without ever missing a word of his sermon; and his joyful addiction to my wife's homemade potato soup. The structure of the friendship that bound our family to him across a long lifetime and in many different settings began in the richness of those early experiences.

By all known means of assessment, Bill Cannon was one of God's unique and unforgettable creations, possessed of a rare and monumental intellect and a gentle, often naively childlike spirit that could be transformed suddenly into an autocratic indignation when provoked; and possessed by his own magnificent obsession to proclaim the good news of Jesus Christ about which he wrote with such colorful candor in his autobiography.

Let me comment briefly on Bishop Cannon from two viewpoints: his widely varied and historic contributions to his church and its ministries; and the fascinating complexities of the man himself as I had opportunity to observe them over a period of more than half a century.

Bishop Cannon served his beloved Methodism as a preacher, teacher, scholar, seminary administrator, episcopal leader and ecumenist. His long career at Emory University began at Emory-at-Oxford in 1942, followed by appointment to the Candler School of Theology faculty a year later, and continuing until his election to the episcopacy in 1968, and then resuming after his retirement as an active bishop in 1984. He served on the faculty of Candler for 25 years and was its dean for 15 years. After he became a bishop, he was made a trustee of the University and later served as vice-chairperson of the Board of Trustees. His term as dean of Candler saw the seminary acquire for its faculty an impressive array of additional distinguished scholars from Europe as well as this country, including its first Jewish member, an internationally known archeologist. He strongly supported Emory's commitment to academic freedom during the "Death of God" furor in the mid-sixties and wrote a low key but brilliant defense of the University for its retention of Dr. Thomas J.J. Altizer, the resident advocate of this position. He guided Candler through the complications of racial integration in the sixties and saw his school begin to emerge as one of the commanding centers for theological education in our denomination and country. During this period, he was in great demand across America as a preacher and lecturer, and had published several highly acclaimed books, including his remarkable work entitled *The Theology of John Wesley*. The impressive 4.8 million dollar chapel on the Emory campus bears his name.

After membership in six General and Jurisdictional Conferences, Dean Cannon was elected a bishop in 1968 and served as the episcopal head of the Raleigh Area (twice), the Atlanta Area and the Richmond Area (when Bishop Herrick was compelled to retire for reasons of health). His unusual personal charisma endeared him to multitudes of clergy and laity in the three episcopal Areas over which he presided. His emphases on Christian education and Christian evangelism became the hallmarks of his administration in all of his annual conferences. He wielded significant influence in the Council of Bishops and was chosen by his colleagues to deliver the Episcopal Address in 1984 during our church's bicentennial observance. It is doubtful if anyone has ever served as a bishop with a richer Biblical and historic understanding of the deep meanings of the office.

Bishop Cannon's long devotion to ecumenism was rooted in his broad knowledge of church history. He became active in the World Methodist Council while he was still at Candler and was one of its moving spirits for decades, serving as a member of the Council Presidium from 1976–1981, and as Chairperson of its Executive Committee from 1981–1986. He was an official observer at the Second Vatican Council and a vigorous participant in the Methodist conversations with Lutheran, Reformed and Roman Catholic scholars and leaders across the years. Along with such distinguished ecumenists as Dr. Joe Hale and the late Dr. Donald English, he became in his own time an almost legendary ambassador from our communion to other branches of the Christian family.

Bill Cannon was by nature a warm, affectionate, modest, caring, gregarious, often humorous, always kind human being. He craved companionship, and spending an evening with him was for many of us a priceless privilege. He was fiercely loyal to his friends—sometimes, his critics said, to a fault.

He had an unusual natural gift for achieving a more than casual relationship with important individuals, something quite understandable because of his brilliant, well-furnished mind, his gracious Southern charm and his Chesterfieldian manners. I never thought he consciously exploited this gift, but rather that the significant contacts resulting from his position frequently elicited eager responses from distinguished personages who found themselves resonating to the Cannon mystique. He was a treasured friend of President and Mrs. Jimmy Carter, offered the prayer at the Carter inauguration, and several times during his travels served as an unofficial envoy for the president, particularly in the tense and troubled Middle East. The Carters joined many other eminent citizens at the bishop's funeral in Atlanta's Northside United Methodist Church in April 1997.

His friendship with Pope John Paul II was widely known. He was the Pope's dinner guest on at least one occasion, and it is reported that John Paul sent him a personal note when he was ill. I recall a time in 1986 when I was introduced to His Holiness, and how there came a twinkle in the papal eyes as he grasped my hand in both of his and asked, "Do you know my friend, Bishop Cannon?" A message from the Pope was read at the funeral.

Bishop Cannon's remarkable mind, equaled only by his great heart, was a storehouse for encyclopedic knowledge, analytical astuteness and artless innocence. I sometimes suspected he used the last to gain admittance to certain chambers of information that otherwise would have been closed to him. His friends were aware that he was not above capitalizing upon the naiveté he knew had been ascribed to him! The bishop was ever the careful, meticulous scholar and, with one exception, the volumes that came from his pen are thoroughly and heavily documented. Following the publication of his delightful *Journeys After Saint Paul*, a sophisticated travelogue written in an enchanting style, I ventured to compliment the book to him, even declaring that I thought it might be the best he had written. He instantly became indignant, responding with almost a trace of anger in his voice, "There's not a single footnote in it!"

The anecdotes about Bishop Cannon are legion, and there are very few, if any, that are apocryphal. Most of them feature one or more of his delicious eccentricities—of which he had an abundance. He was aware of these stories and seemed to enjoy hearing them. Once, when he had presented me to speak at a session of the Virginia

Conference, he stopped me on my way to the podium and asked me to tell a certain tale about him during my address.

Bill Cannon was a wealthy man by inheritance and through wise investments, but he lived modestly, even frugally. His one extravagance was travel. But he was, in a very remarkable way, a generous person who did his philanthropy almost secretly. His very substantial gifts to Yale (for the restoration of the quadrangle) and Emory (for the chapel building fund) were known only to a few of his friends. Once, very quietly, he said to me, "I have just finished paying for the higher education of my one-hundredth student." His very large gift to Candler by bequest was designated mainly for student scholarships.

His own "life-conquering, death-conquering faith," to use the powerful words of his dearest friend, Bishop Mack B. Stokes, in his magnificent funeral eulogy, was Bishop Cannon's most conspicuous and compelling characteristic. It was a faith informed by a vast knowledge, interpreted by one of the brightest minds the church has ever known, and matured through a lifelong discipline of Bible study and prayer. Wesleyan to the core, his was a classical orthodoxy, articulated always with logic and passion.

William Ragsdale Cannon, Jr. was in many ways a contemporary counterpart of the great patristic figures from those early centuries he knew so well, but he was also a thoroughly modern, completely fascinating, sometimes delightfully funny, nearly irresistible friend and companion. His preaching and lecturing were alive with picturesque historical allusions, vivid and warm human interest stories and unexpected humor. He brought almost incredible gifts to United Methodism and to twentieth century Christianity. The church may not see his like again.

His was a friendship I did not deserve, but for which I am eternally grateful.

Edmund W. Robb, Jr.

This address was delivered in Dallas, Texas, on the evening of July 20, 1994, when Dr. Robb's official retirement was celebrated by a large company of his friends from across the nation.

Edmund W. Robb, Jr., deliberately selected what he knew would be an extremely controversial life and career. His basic work was that of an evangelist, traceable to his dramatic conversion to Christianity in Glide Memorial Church in San Francisco, but he elected to build into this ministry an insistence upon aspects of church reform which he regarded as necessary if the Christian Faith was to survive and prosper in our time. In this role he elicited for himself a deluge of criticisms which he always managed to handle with grace, fairness and Christian charity toward his opponents. As I attempted to say in this address, he was a totally honest and utterly loyal United Methodist and was often more tolerant of his critics than they were of him.

One of the most curious partnerships and friendships in the history of the modern church was that which developed between Dr. Robb and Dr. Albert Outler, the famous theologian. It was this which eventuated in the organization of A Foundation for Theological Education—an agency (actually a movement) which has resulted in bringing influential evangelical enrichment to theological education as a new century has begun. This, a genuinely remarkable achievement, is the principal Robb legacy to his beloved United Methodism.

Edmund W. Robb, Jr.

"Isn't it strange that princes and kings
And clowns that caper in sawdust rings
And ordinary folk like you and me
Are builders of Eternity[1]?"

I am honored to be asked to deliver an address commemorating the life and ministry of one of the most courageous and loyal United Methodist clergypersons I have ever known, who is also my dear friend. No one can begin to understand and appreciate Ed Robb without being aware of the basic breadth and charity which help to define his strong and independent character and personality. The historic friendship which developed between Dr. Robb and the late Dr. Albert Outler is dramatic documentation of this fact. And it is only because of such native capacity for bigness, such unfailing hospitality to fairness and objectivity, that the accomplishments of any leader, even those of Dr. Robb, can have the quality of permanence. It would be quite safe to say that he is unlike many of his critics at this point.

It was Nicholas Murray Butler, sometime President of Columbia University, who reminded us that there are three kinds of people: those who don't know what is happening, those who know but do nothing about it, and those who know and <u>do</u> something about it! Edmund W. Robb, Jr. has lived and worked under the rubric of Dr. Butler's third group. I propose to speak about our honoree as an evangelist, as a United Methodist, as one of the two founders of A Foundation for Theological Education (AFTE) and as a person.

An Evangelist

The final recorded public statement of John R. Mott, Methodism's most famous lay person in this century, was a single sentence uttered by him at the last meeting of the Central Committee of the World Council of Churches which he attended: "Let it be remembered that John R. Mott was an evangelist!"

This would be an appropriate affirmation for Ed Robb to make when, hopefully years from now, his ministerial career is about to be concluded. If someone were to attempt a single word description of Dr. Robb, that word would need to be "evangelist."

He has had numerous other roles in the Christian community: pastor, author, fund-raiser, editor, crusader, trustee, etc. But always, and in all roles, he has kept on being an evangelist. In preparing this address, I inquired about the number of revivals or preaching missions that he has held, the number of decisions for Christ that have come as a result of his preaching, and the number of young people who have volunteered for full-time service in response to his plea. I was really not surprised to learn that he has never kept numerical records, and these figures simply are not available. This is in keeping with what I know about him. He has sought always to glorify his Savior, and not himself. However, anyone familiar with the scope of his ministry and the congestion of his calendar would agree that he has led literally thousands into the presence of Jesus Christ, and that hundreds of young people have come under his influence in making their decisions for Christian service.

It is not difficult to analyze the Robb affinity for evangelistic effort. He takes the mandates of the Bible and historic Christianity with the utmost seriousness. The powerful memory of his own conversion causes him to covet similar experiences for others. He loves people, and has the enviable ability to see in them what God sees. Beyond all of this, the practicality of his churchmanship causes him to know that the Christian faith's primary task is to enable the Holy Spirit to transform and redirect human life. He surely is not against social change for the betterment of the human family and the enactment of laws to compliment this, but he is convinced that no structure of law built upon the teachings of Jesus can long endure if it is not supported by a public which has been converted to Christ and His way of life.

Ed Robb is a preacher—a preacher whose pulpit utterances have a quality of their own beyond any special emphasis, but whose sermons are always intentionally evangelistic. They reflect careful study and research, and give evidence of much reading. Their content is substantive and sound, but Dr. Robb, like Tennyson's scholar, "wears his weight of learning lightly as a flower." There is always clear logic, for this is the way his mind works. Someone said of Warren G. Harding's speeches: "They are an army of pompous phrases moving ponderously over the landscape in search of an idea." The antithesis would be true of Dr. Robb's public addresses.

His preaching demonstrates real fundamentalism, although he himself could never be called a fundamentalist. There is always a strong emphasis upon the basics of religion, no fluff, no window dressing, no jargon. Dr. Robb knows how to preach for a verdict, how to close the sale, how to convince his hearers that a response is required *now*.

A special authenticity belongs to Ed Robb's evangelistic efforts because of his extended experience as pastor of local churches, including St. Paul in Midland and St. Luke in Lubbock. Any evangelism insensitive to the needs of the local congregation is suspect in the eyes of church leadership, and rightly so. Dr. Robb's soul-winning enterprises are always designed to build the church, and his evangelism is accomplished within a strong pastoral context.

Ed Robb is a *spiritual* person in the very best sense of the word. One of his close friends, with whom I consulted as I developed this message, spoke with appreciation about his unwavering confidence in those beliefs which he preaches. Another mentioned that he has a "relationship with God that is absolutely honest and true." These are important evaluations, for they assure us that the Robb evangelism operates out of a frame of reference infinitely larger than itself. He knows God and trusts Him to give his human words the wings of the morning and the touch of Heaven's power. George Arthur Buttrick said once that a sermon is an offering a preacher makes to God. I am confident that this accurately describes Dr. Rob's philosophy of the pulpit. He knows that "God gives the increase." Whatever work of redemption occurs in an individual or a congregation, it is always the gift of the Holy Spirit. Dr. Robb is fully aware that no preacher, no evangelist himself or herself ever saved anyone.

A Loyal United Methodist

A friend of mine who is a well-known American educator tells about a certain distinguished president of a great university who said to his young successor, "In my desk, you will find two envelopes; open each as indicated." The first one had written on the outside of it "When you are in *serious* trouble," and the second "When you are in *desperate* trouble." As the story goes, after a year, the young president decided that the moment had come to open the first of the two envelopes left him by his predecessor. Within it, he found a slip of paper on which was written, "Blame it on me." One and one-half years later, he was forced to decide that his plight fitted the caption of the second envelope, and so he opened it. A slip of paper there contained these words, "Make out two envelopes."

Dr. Robb has never found himself in the position of that troubled university president. In spite of his grim awareness of the colossal problems which afflict human society and mainline Protestantism in the 1990s, he has never surrendered the kind of confidence in the future which rests back upon the greatness and goodness of Almighty God. Many years ago, Mary Martin sang a lilting song in the Broadway musical "South Pacific" in which there appeared two lines that aptly describe the Robb perspective:

> "I'm stuck like a dope
> with a thing called hope."

The role of a prophet from Biblical times until now is to define dramatically the things that are wrong and alien to God's will in human life and organized religion at any given time. This does not mean that the prophet is either a pessimist or an iconoclast. Nor does it mean that he or she lacks compassion or tenderness. Critics, for their own reasons, often accuse such a prophet of all these things, but history, if the prophet's heart is pure, usually will render a different verdict. Ed Robb's quarrel with the church, like my own and that of many others here tonight, has always been a lover's quarrel. I know of no minister in all of United Methodism who loves his or her church more than he does. He would be comfortable nowhere else.

Brother Ed, while still serving in the United States Navy during the World War II era gave his heart to the Lord under the preaching of Dr. Julian C. McPheeters at the old Glide Memorial Methodist Church in San Francisco. It was a complicated odyssey from that long ago service to his participation in the Oxford Institute in 1982 and his prominent role in designing two scholarly colloquies at Notre Dame University. But throughout the journey, no one who has really known Edmund W. Robber, Jr. has had reason to question his stalwart loyalty to historic Wesleyan religion and The United Methodist Church. I often fear that there are some good people whose bitter cynicism actually would cause them to deplore the emergence of successful efforts to set our church's house in order, but Ed Robb would never find himself a member of such a company. Rather, he would be in the vanguard of those leading the hallelujahs!

Our church is in a theological, or more precisely a Christological, crisis tonight. To acknowledge this fact is neither treason nor alarmism. It can be the highest form of loyalty and love. God help us to be grateful for a person like Dr. Robb whose honest realism has pioneered a new ecclesiastical morning of promise and hope.

A Founder of AFTE

I happen to have been in his audience on that Summer night in 1975 when Dr. Robb delivered his powerful polemic against contemporary theological education at Lake Junaluska. Its strength and eloquence sprang from the informed indignation of a dedicated Christian who was convinced that in many instances our seminaries, instead of building the church and enabling its gospel, were actually endangering the faith and zeal of its ministry. The address was well-researched, and the speaker made his point with dramatic clarity. The seminary community and its leadership reacted with righteously angry resistance, and Professor Albert Outler, Perkins School of Theology, Southern Methodist University was one of those who became most articulate in his response to the Robb indictment. It was his article in *The United Methodist Reporter* which led Dr. Robb to seek a face-to-face interview with the famous Wesleyan theologian in his office on the university campus. Because both men were honest and fair-minded, an enduring, if curious, friendship began. Dr. Robb, in his Lake Junaluska address, had deplored the virtual absence of evangelical voices in the faculties of our United Methodist theological schools; and Dr. Outler, upon reflection, agreed that this was a sad but true analysis of the situation. Robb and Outler, both bold activists, began to see what the latter, writing in *The Christian Century*, February 6–13, 1980, referred to as "a Heaven-sent opportunity."

In a few months, *A Foundation for Theological Education* was born. I shall never forget the day when Professor Outler telephoned me in my Nashville office and, exercising his incredible persuasive powers, enlisted me to be a charter member of AFTE's Board of Trustees, an office I am still honored to hold.

Now, seventeen years later, seventy John Wesley Fellows,[1] representing the most brilliant evangelical minds in the current Christian community, have been trained for their terminal degrees at world famous universities here and abroad, their expenses underwritten by this Foundation. This million-dollar plus enterprise has resulted in the placement of nearly forty intellectually formidable proponents of historic Wesleyan doctrine in seminaries and colleges across our land.[2] Some of these dedicated scholars have already attained national and even international distinction, and have made a substantial and exciting impact upon the quality of ministerial training in our time.

Drs. Robb and Outler were the inspiration for this remarkable project. Dr. Robb has been its ongoing advocate and organizational genius, and has procured the multiplied hundreds of thousands of dollars necessary to fund its program.

Speaking about him in this last-named role, a mutual friend once said to me with sanguine resignation, "When Dr. Robb discovers you, it's always simpler just to go ahead and write a check." Every ex-college president, like myself, is a weary alumnus of the exalted order of professional extractors of money from the sometimes reticent wealthy, but few have been as successful as this Texas evangelist. He is the financial catalyst for one of the most thrilling adventures in the realm of theological education our church has ever known.

Let me note here two things. Ed Robb, always driven by his rugged Texas common sense, would be critical of some of higher education's indefensible facades. Even though it does not represent his (or my) creation or belief, he probably would chuckle about the kind of teacher described in these four lines of doggerel:

> "First he was a tadpole beginning to begin,
> Then he was a frog with his tail tucked in,
> Next he was a monkey hanging from a tree,
> Finally he was a professor with a Ph.D."

But it is very important to declare that Ed Robb, as I have known him, is a dedicated devotee to the very best in higher learning. This may be true in part because he was never privileged to pursue his own formal education beyond the baccalaureate level. Consequently, he has devoted the years of his ministry to an eager and relentless pursuit of self-education, reading avidly and widely, and acquiring by mental osmosis the richness of knowledge and wisdom possessed by scholars whom he has met and known.

One other statement should be made: Dr. Robb is a serious and sincere friend of theological education, and of the United Methodist seminary. The deeper meaning of AFTE centers in its proud realization of the fundamental and prior importance of a well-trained ministry, grounded in basics of theological truth and designed to enable an ordained person, preaching in this sophisticated age, "to give a reason for the faith that is in him or her."

When a national committee chose Dr. Edmund W. Robb, Jr. as one of the "Forty Distinguished Evangelists" of the Methodist world to be installed in the Hall of Fame of The Foundation for Evangelism, the chairperson said to me, "We had to include him because of his role in establishing AFTE! This is one of the most important achievements for our church in the last half century."

A Person

All of us occasionally feel a sense of deep indebtedness to a host of good people who have helped conserve values precious to us. Tonight we have focused not upon the many, but upon a single individual.

Dr. Robb, before he became an evangelist, a crusader for a renewed denomination, or a founder of a great movement related to theological education, was a person, an individual whose life has been touched uniquely with God's presence and power.

People with whom I talked as I prepared for this occasion used such adjectives as "enthusiastic," "likable," "honest," and such phrases as "confident in his faith" and "always understanding if a person has other causes in which he or she is interested." I could add testimony about his charity and gentle spiritedness toward those who disagree with him—alas, sometimes many. All of this speaks vividly of a broadly gauged human being, a person with a roomy soul and a huge sense of fairness.

Here is a case in point. A minister and his wife had a son going through the agonies of latent rebellion and personal confusion, without anchors of Christian commitment, alone in a great city. By accident (or Providence!), Dr. Robb met him and a friendship between the two, nurtured carefully and intentionally by this rugged Texas preacher, began. It persisted across many months and numerous expensive meals hosted by Ed Robb when he happened to visit that city. He never once tried to thrust his religion upon his new friend, but simply allowed the Holy Spirit to use the love and concern with which he surrounded this young man.

Now, years later, both the parents and the son know that the renaissance of sanity and faith which came to the young man was induced, under God, by the skillful evangelism and wise tactfulness of Ed Robb.

No one can ever analyze Ed Robb's career adequately without paying a deep and sincere tribute to his lovely wife Martha. Now pursuing her own important career in municipal government, she has surrounded her husband with unfailing love, understanding and wisdom across forty-seven years of marriage.

But let us take care lest our adulation become too extravagant. Dr. Robb is human, very human. He likes blackeyed peas and cornbread, a fact that may not enhance his cultural coefficient. It is said that he sometimes decides not to drink coffee for a period of time as a kind of exercise in spiritual discipline, but I am confidently informed that somewhere along the way he may begin drinking a substitute product called Brim, even though he is constantly boasting to his friends that he has stopped his intake of caffeine.

Ed and Martha have five children, two of whom are journalists. The other three are involved in the Christian ministry. When they were very young, there is a story about their rowdiness in a roadside café somewhere between Midland and Austin, which embarrassed their parents to the point where Ed engineered his family's abrupt departure. A couple of miles down the road, they discovered that they had left the baby in its bassinet in the café, and had to turn around. After a fairly heated discussion about which parent would go into the restaurant to get the baby, an argument Ed lost, the Texas evangelist marched silently and with as much dignity as he could muster into the café to claim their child. It may be hard to imagine tonight's distinguished honoree, now a doting grandfather, in such a compromising situation—but I assure you that I have verified the authenticity of this story.

Enough of such foolishness! However, I assure you that the repertoire is not exhausted!

One final word. This evening of celebration of a man's ministry comes at a chaotic moment in time. The headlines and telecasts have reverberated with messages about Bosnia, Rwanda, Haiti, the Korean peninsula, Russia and a dangerous zealot named Zhirinovsky, the United States with the sad episode of Tonya Harding, and the court cases of the Menendez brothers, the Bobbitts and O. J. Simpson. One does not deal with violent evil by making sure that the response is "politically correct"—although this seems too often the practice of today's stereotypical church leaders in confronting ecclesiastical issues that may be quite as serious as political or criminal matters. Forthright courage, tempered with wisdom, is required whether the problem at hand belongs to secular culture or the community of faith.

There is a quaint story about Bishop Edwin Holt Hughes eating breakfast in a Pullman diner with Dr. Henry Clay Morrison half a century ago. The train lurched abruptly, and Dr. Morrison found his immaculate white shirt suddenly stained with the yolk of his morning egg. Bishop Hughes, always quick to see humor, commented, "No one would ever say that the color yellow belongs anywhere on your person, Dr. Morrison!" Nor could anyone ever say that yellow belongs anywhere in the vicinity of Edmund W. Robb, Jr. His ministry, praise God, has never been inhibited by cowardice or political correctness.

It was George Bernard Shaw who said, "A gentleman is one who contributes more to the common trust than he takes out." We have saluted this distinguished Christian evangelist, our friend and brother, who is a true gentleman in the Shavian sense. We thank Almighty God for the integrity of his life and the power of his witness. He would wish us to close this evening with the assurance that all that all of us have said has sought not to glorify him, but rather to bring honor to the Name of the One who is the fairest among ten thousand and altogether lovely, his Lord and Savior, and ours!

Endnotes

1   R. Lee Sharpe, "A Bag of Tools"; from James Dalton Morrison, *Masterpieces of Religious Verse*: New York, Harper and Brothers, 1948.

2   The number now (2005) is over 100.

3   AFTE scholars now head two of our most prominent seminaries and a variety of this select group, some internationally recognized, are on the faculties of a number of our seminaries. One AFTE scholar, Dr. Scott Jones, was elected a bishop in 2004 and assigned to Kansas.

IX

On Both Sides of The Iron Curtain

This is the formal report which I made to the Council of Bishops in November 1970 following my summer travels in Germany and Austria. There are three particular memories either not mentioned or not adequately described in the text of this document.

The first is four days of hospitalization in the Martha-Mary Hospital (a German Methodist institution) in Munich, operated by the incomparable German deaconesses, where I was treated like royalty for the principal reason that I had, on one of those days, a daily devotional in the German translation of The Upper Room. *I can still see a group of six nurses coming to the door of my room, holding up a copy of that publication, and pointing their fingers at me!*

The second memory is about the famous German superhighways called the autobahns where there is <u>no</u> speed limit. My young German clerical escorts assigned by Bishop Sommer found quite early that while my family took this phenomenon in stride, I had a massive fear that almost overcame me when we deliberately drove on these roads. I learned later that this was such good sport for our young preachers that they telephoned each other at night and planned to subject the visiting bishop to the most monumental fear possible the following day!

The third memory is about Bavarian homemade potato soup—one of my favorite foods in any country. I complained near the end of our visit in that part of Germany that I had not had any of that celebrated soup while there, and was told that German hosts and hostesses did not serve it to guests. That night my good friends made an exception in my case and invited me to their parsonage for participation in a pot of soup so memorable that I can still taste it!

The value of this selection, now thirty-five years old, may be that it constitutes a fragment of European church history. This would be particularly true of the part describing our special mission in East Germany.

On Both Sides of The Iron Curtain

An Introductory Word

Mrs. Hunt, our son Stephen (21 years of age and a rising senior in college) and I spent the entire month of July touring United Methodism in Germany and, very briefly, Austria. Since our official assignment was to visit the Frankfurt Area and most of our itinerary was within the boundaries of this Area, I shall confine my report principally to German Methodism.

As we all know, after World War II the country was divided into the Federal Republic of Germany (West Germany) and the German Democratic Republic (East Germany), with the great, sprawling city of Berlin situated in the heart of the Communist segment but itself split into two non-communicating halves. Efforts on the part of the post-war occupying powers to effect even the beginnings of reunion have failed, but within the past few months overtures on the part of the German governments themselves may be in the process of ushering into existence not organic reunion but at least a more tolerable relationship.

It should be stated that the more realistic citizens of West Germany whom we met, and the few East Germans we were privileged to know, seem to have accepted the fact that there are now *two nations*, and in all probability will be for the foreseeable future. Reason seems about to win out over emotion and heartbreak at this point. We saw the Wall in Berlin—from both sides. We saw also the bleak barbed wire fence with its ominous signs of warning and its grim armed guards bisecting the lovely countryside, particularly at the point of a beautiful beach on the Baltic Sea, and we had our own vivid impressions of the traumatic contrast between freedom and policed oppression.

A Special Assignment

Our assignment did not include a study of Methodism in East Germany, and our observations about the German people and the German churches must of necessity be confined primarily to what we were able to see and understand during approximately one month of visitation in the Federal Republic of Germany. At the request of the Council of Bishops and the General Council on Finance and Administration, we arranged to visit East Berlin for the express purpose of meeting and welcoming into the Council of Bishops the Reverend Dr. Armin Härtel, who had been elected to the episcopacy by the Methodist Church in East Germany two or three weeks prior to our arrival. We were privileged to be the first family in the American episcopacy to have contact with Bishop Härtel in his new position. He came to East Berlin for the particular purpose of meeting us. Bishop Sommer, in a way we never learned, communicated with Superintendent Emeritus Johannes Falk who lived in East Germany, and requested him to meet us as we entered East Berlin and accompany us during the day. We were escorted on our mission by a brilliant young West German pastor who had limited liaison with the East Germans and who drove us in his car. We sought access to East Berlin through the celebrated Checkpoint Charlie. As we came to the entrance booths we were stopped for prolonged questioning and were finally approved to go into East Berlin. It was quite apparent to me that Bishop Härtel was already under surveillance by the East German officials and that there was serious inquiry into all of his travels and his personal contacts. We had been advised by Bishop Sommer not to undertake visitation of any of our churches in East Berlin, and upon counsel of Superintendent Falk and upon counsel of our clerical escort, reinforced by the judgment of Superintendent Falk, we planned to have our meeting with Bishop Härtel in the famous Pergamon Museum. We found him waiting for us and exchanged the amenities of introduction and greeting, all of us attempting to assume the identity of tourists simply engaged in a normal visit to a great sight-seeing attraction.

As we strolled casually through some of the rooms of the museum, we came upon a magnificent statue of Hammurabi, the Babylonian lawgiver. It seemed to afford us a kind of secluded place for our first substantive conversation with Bishop Härtel. I extended the welcome of the Council of Bishops to him and, as unobtrusively as possible, placed in his hands the briefing documents I had been asked to give to him. He put them in his briefcase, and it was at that moment that we became aware of two or three other persons standing nearby whom we instantly identified as East German surveillance officers. It was an open question how much they had overheard of our conversation, but we felt that the first part of it must have been completed before their appearance. We tried to resume the role of tourists and made a brief tour of the great museum. Then Bishop Härtel joined the four of us in our driver's automobile and we made our way to a large restaurant for lunch. When we were seated, the same individuals whom we had seen in the Pergamon Museum came in and requested to be seated at a table nearby. This, of course, made it unwise for us to continue our official conversation, and we spent a rather uncomfortable time eating a meal of questionable quality and talking about what we had seen in the museum. Our driver, who knew East Berlin quite well, suggested that we ought to visit the Soviet War Memorial. This destination, when we reached it, seemed to perplex our unwelcome East German companions, and they permitted us, surprisingly, an unexpected period of privacy during which we completed our visit with Bishop Härtel and bade him farewell.

It remained for us to make our exit from East Berlin through Checkpoint Charlie back to the comfortable friendliness on the other side of the Iron Curtain. However, we encountered a three-hour delay at the departure booths, where, to our great surprise, the guards confronted us with amazingly accurate profiles of the Hunt family, Superintendent Falk and our clerical driver. They took my camera from me, removed the film and destroyed it. They seated us in a small adjoining room and left us to ponder what might happen. About two hours later we caught a glimpse of the three men who had followed us during the earlier part of the day, and Superintendent Falk and our ministerial escort overheard them tell the guards about our visit to the Soviet War Museum. Apparently this bit of information saved us from a much longer delay at Checkpoint Charlie. One of the guards came into the room where we were and motioned for us to get into our car and drive to the other side of the Wall. Thus it was that we returned to the security of West Berlin and were able to declare our special mission accomplished.

The Church in West Germany

As the cradle of the Reformation, Germany has continued through the years to be a focal point in the Christian world for Biblical scholarship and theological reflection. Its organized religious life earned an authentic and honored place in the annals of Christian courage during the desperate years of Hitler's rule when "the churches were the main nuclei of spiritual resistance to the dominant Nazi power."[1] This stance, taken at such high cost by the German churches, was dramatized in retrospect for me as we stood for a little while during our special mission one day this past summer in East Berlin's celebrated *Marienkirche* (Church of Saint Mary) and I gazed up at the massively ornate pulpit from which the late Bishop Otto Dibelius had so often proclaimed religious freedom and the judgment of God upon all forms of human tyranny.

Against the backdrop of our knowledge of the Christian religion's prominent role in German history, early and late, we found it difficult to assimilate the fact that members of the state-supported Lutheran Church had virtually ceased attendance upon its public worship. We were told that the percentage of participation in Sunday services was as low as two or three. We knew, of course, of the hopeful emergence of German lay academies, developed after 1945 under the leadership of Doctors Eberhard Mueller and Helmut Thielicke, and of their significant Christian impact upon the secularized post-war culture. But we still found it difficult to reconcile ourselves to the pathetically small attendance in the splendid and historic churches of Hamburg, Cologne, Frankfurt am Main, Stuttgart, Nurnberg and Munich (places and edifices which we visited ourselves).

We were delighted, on the other hand, to learn of the vigor characterizing life in the Free Churches: United Methodist, Baptist, Free Congregationalist, Mennonite, Lutheran Free Church, Old Catholic Church and Salvation Army. Our own study had to be confined, of course, to the Methodist churches. Springing from two important parent streams, British and American (united in 1896), Methodism in the Federal Republic comprises four annual conferences: South (three districts), Southwest (two districts), Northwest (three districts) and West Berlin (one district). Together these annual conferences compose the Frankfurt Area and the West Germany Central Conference under the able episcopal leadership of Bishop C. Ernst Sommer, educator and minister, himself the son of another distinguished and beloved German bishop. German Methodism, springing from modest evangelistic beginnings under Christoph Gottlieb Mueller in Southern Germany in 1832, grew under the inspired labors of dedicated Methodist Christians like William Nast (longtime editor of the beloved German-language paper *The Christian Apologist*), Lewis S. Jacoby, Erhard and Frederick Wunderlich, Lewis Nippert (founder of Methodist theological training in Germany, whose first school in Bremen later was moved to Frankfurt to become the important seminary which still stands as a beacon in European theological study) and the famous Bishop John L. Neulsen, distinguished on both sides of the Atlantic. In the difficult struggles of the past quarter of a century, the names of Bishop Frederick Wunderlich, the two Bishops Sommer, Bishop Arthur J. Moore and Bishop Paul N. Garber have become indissolubly associated with the emergence of the strong and significant church which exists today. While the membership of approximately 100,000 is small in comparison to American Methodist numerical strength (being not much more than 1-1/100th of the latter), it is of importance to note that the memberships in the two countries are more nearly equalized by the fact that 75% of German Methodist members attend services regularly and participate in church activities. Vast numbers tithe their incomes, thus enabling a modestly-sized church with very little affluence to support a strong program with responsibility for approximately *sixty* institutions.

Salaries of West German Methodist pastors have been equalized basically (with appropriate gradations to care for differing family responsibilities, seniority, etc.), but are almost unbelievably low in terms of our salaries. The maximum amount a German Methodist minister may earn per month is 1,020 D.M. (1,220 D.M. for a district superintendent)—or never as much as $4,500 per year in American money! Parsonages, nearly always located in the same buildings which house the churches, are provided in addition to salary, and there is a reasonably adequate retirement program. A few churches subsidize automobile costs for their ministers. Ministerial appointments apparently are made after full consultation and ordinarily are released quite early. We spoke with several ministers who were concluding service in their present churches and knew precisely what their next appointments would be, thus enabling them to make both emotional and practical adjustments to removal of residence.

We found a genuinely pure but unostentatious pietism characterizing German United Methodism. It seemed to be prominent in the perspective of ministers and in the expectation of parishioners. It was not a superficial pietism but rather a deeper qualitative reality which expressed itself, almost always with humility, in commitment. Our own analysis of German Methodist pietism brought us to the conclusion that it is essentially Bible-based, and reflects the universal emphasis of German clergy and laity alike upon the fundamental role of the Holy Scriptures in the life of the church and the Christian community. German Methodist churches, we discovered, are not overly eager to hear American Methodist preachers for the plain and simple reason that they have discovered these men and women are not essentially Bible preachers! Exegesis and exposition are homiletical ground rules in the German pulpit. But it is not a narrow, bigoted, schismatic, fundamentalistic Bibliolatry. Rather, it is a scholarly, even critical, approach which represents the finest and purest viewpoints available in the contemporary church.

One searching for meaningful Christian activism in the life of the German United Methodist Church would be somewhat perplexed, if not wholly disappointed, if his or her quest were confined to the seven centers and approximately seventy local congregations or edifices which we visited. The emphasis is upon personal religion, but the implication is that this personal religion will be expressed in constructive and progressive citizenship and in a correct perspective on social and community issues. We discovered several of the ministers, particularly two of them, to have sensitive social consciences and to be engaged vigorously in efforts to make the institutional church knowledgeable and articulate in various areas of human perplexity—with special concern for the anxieties of youth.

The public services which we were privileged to attend were well-conducted and very worshipful. Liturgical ornateness was never in evidence, and I was warned before leaving America that it would be better if I did not plan to wear either a pulpit gown or clericals. Part of this present mood is traceable, I believe, to the recent merger of German Methodism and the small but vigorous Evangelical and United Brethren contingent in that country.

The institutions of German United Methodism are outstanding. We visited numerous hospitals, operated by the marvelous and skillful German United Methodist Deaconesses, youth hostels, Deaconess Mother Houses and Evening Houses, really magnificent homes and apartments for the retired, unique "social institutions" (as they are called in Germany) which are in fact lovely vacation resorts owned and operated by the church for Christian clienteles, and the very impressive and financially successful Publishing House in Stuttgart. Measuring my language with care, I would have to say that each institution we saw seemed to be clearly outstanding in its own way. Quite remarkable business acumen and fidelity to sound financial principles result in these institutions costing church members a minimum in economic subsidy.

All in all, we discovered German United Methodism to be an extremely vigorous and proud component of The United Methodist Church, in some ways a serious rebuke to those of us who belong to that church in the United States of America.

Austrian Methodism

Our visit to Austria was brief and less official than the assignment in Germany, but I must record clear and important impressions regarding the quality of our church's work in that country. We went first to Vienna and were privileged to visit several churches there, as well as the very interesting and well-operated vacation home on the outskirts of the city. I spent a day in Linz, under the escort of the Reverend Helmut Nausner, son of the almost legendary couple, Poppa and Momma Nausner, so intimately identified with Austrian and European Methodism over a long period of years. In addition to visiting his church and parsonage, Brother Nausner took me in particular to see the operation of the well-known Methodist kindergarten project associated with his church. This effort, meeting a genuine need in the city and giving the church's work there a significant influence upon people far beyond the Methodist community, had to be moved out of quarters no longer safe for occupancy and the congregation, in a magnificent gesture of sacrifice, moved themselves into the upstairs or attic portion of their building, where they improvised a sanctuary, permitting the kindergarten project to take over the more spacious public quarters on the ground floor where previously all services of the church had been held. I have never encountered a more selfless devotion to a church's mission of community service than was here evident.

I visited also in Linz the very unusual and remarkable Methodist Home for Christian Rehabilitation of young ladies who have had some minor problem with the law. The superintendent of this large and impressive project is one of the three outstanding architects of Switzerland who experienced Christian conversion and thereupon redirected his life into this particular channel of church-related service. He and his wife were host and hostess to an unforgettable noontime meal in the Home, at which I was privileged to meet guests from America and also Poppa and Momma Nausner, who came down to Linz for that occasion. I was particularly glad to have this exposure to these projects in Linz in view of the fact that my own annual conference had already committed itself to financial assistance for their ongoing requirements.

I may say simply and briefly that we were impressed with two things in particular about Austrian Methodism. The first is its numerical or statistical weakness, making any larger impact something of wonder. Second, I was delighted to note the unusually happy marriage of pietism and activism in this small but vigorous church. We were impressed with the Biblical basis of the church's thought, study and worship. But it seemed to me that this Biblical foundation served everywhere as a firm floor for a structure of meaningful involvement in societal needs and problems, giving the little Methodist community much wider influence in the State than could be understood apart from this factor. All in all, Austrian United Methodism and the people we were privileged to meet within it were an inspiration to our family.

In Conclusion

I must say, for my family and myself, a final word of deep and abiding appreciation for our German and Austrian friends and for the warm and gracious hospitality which everywhere surrounded us during our odyssey abroad. To try to sum up the religious impact of the trip upon my own spirit would be difficult indeed, but I think I might say that we saw in German United Methodism a people with a long, long view of Faith. They have passed through two World Wars, through defeat and destruction, through shame and humiliation. Nowhere did we find supreme importance attached to a building program or, for that matter, to bricks and mortar themselves. Their concept of the church is that it is something infinitely more than architecture and edifices. Material prosperity, the achievement of paid-up budgets, is not as important to them as it is to us. The church to our German Methodist friends seems to be a spiritual entity, the household of faith. They are a minority group, even in the Christian community of their own country, but they are vibrantly and vitally alive. The eschatological perspective is implicit in their thought, their preaching and their living—born certainly of the almost apocalyptic ordeals through which they have passed in recent years. It is an intelligent and informed eschatology, characteristic of the splendidly furnished German mind. The German Methodists have the joyful assurance that they are living in what the late D. T. Niles loved to call "the passive voice." He put it beautifully in one of his last books: "At home, I live as a person who is loved by my wife and by my children. My family is conscious of the same feeling. The children do not get up in the morning and say, 'We must today love father and mother.' *They simply live as those who are loved....*"[2]

German United Methodists, devoted to the Holy Bible and acutely conscious of the Holy Spirit, regard the Christian faith as of God. They are conscious of its vertical dimension *before* they deal with its horizontal obligation—but they would insist that the former does not impede the latter. Their faith, for themselves, their church and the entirety of the Christian enterprise, is in Him. *To employ a theological term, they are living their religion as glorious prolepsis—the assumption that its future power is even now a present reality.* And so it sustains them. They are kept by its vision and secured by its promise. Perhaps we cannot understand the vigor and the power of the tiny German United Methodist Church apart from understanding their perspective at this point. And perhaps for American United Methodists, propelled by activistic idealism, such understanding will come hard.

It was a wonderful trip, in spite of autobahns and the absence of ice water! In 1889 Mark Twain wrote the story of a Hartford citizen in Camelot, a piece of historical fiction called *A Connecticut Yankee in King Arthur's Court.* So, with just as much incongruity, I have been an American churchman in the courts of Charlemagne and Willy Brandt! And with a heart still warm because of a strange land's gracious hospitality to my family and myself, I have returned, as I went, a glad learner, seeking to report what I saw and felt. And may the grace of the Lord Jesus Christ be with all of that splendid company of United Methodist people in the Federal Republic of Germany!

X

Through Lenses of Hope

This was a State of the Church address prepared and delivered at the Florida Annual Conference in June 1987, one and one-quarter years before my official retirement from the active episcopacy. It was my custom to present such a document at the beginning of each of the annual conference sessions over which I presided. There are two particular reasons for the reproduction of this text here. The first is its detailed discussion of the appointment-making process as it is affected by consultations, a matter quite new for United Methodism and ordered by the General Conference. This extremely valuable procedure is still undergoing refinement now, many years after it became mandatory.

The second is its description of the manner in which a great annual conference was able to address with total success a very unfortunate and very large indebtedness to itself. Here I must make an extremely important point. It was not the practice of Florida's episcopal leadership to inquire deeply into basic fiscal matters. My two predecessors, both warm personal friends, were men of unquestionable integrity and honor, and their administrations had been signally effective. When I came along, as a former college president, I was curious about balance sheets and particularly sensitive to any innocent misuse of dedicated funds. Our treasurer was a splendid Christian layman, totally honest and eager to provide funding for conference programs. For some reason the Conference Council on Finance and Administration had not challenged the practices that resulted in use of designated funds for undesignated purposes. It was a situation for which there was no intentional blame to be placed on anyone, but a set of circumstances which I felt a very keen obligation to change.

This address records the remarkable greatness of a magnificent annual conference and its deeply dedicated lay people.

Through Lenses of Hope

Text: *"And Joshua said unto the people, Sanctify yourselves; for tomorrow the Lord will do wonders among you."* (Joshua 3:5)

This lovely statement from the early portion of one of the great historical works of the Old Testament is buoyant with an expectancy that Joshua, overflowing with confidence, sought to build into the people—an expectancy dependent upon the prior fact of the people's inner preparation to receive the blessings of Heaven. At the heart of our holy religion today as in the far-off yesterdays, in spite of Iran and Iraq, apartheid in South Africa, Gary Hart and the Fourth Estate, Iranscam, Gorbachev's "glasnost," tremblings in the Philippines, Jim and Tammy Bakker, AIDS and Alzheimer's, there is still the persistent message of *hope*. It is more needed now than ever before in our century, and more difficult to come by. The late Dr. Joseph Sizoo put our choice clearly when he referred to Charles Kingsley's *Waterbabies*, reminding us that there is *Epimetheus*, always looking back, caught up in his memory of the "good old days," and there is *Prometheus*, looking forward constantly, interested only in the future and believing that God has great things in store for future years. Between the attitudes of Epimetheus and Prometheus each of us has to make his or her choice; we live either with one or the other. Living with Prometheus and hope requires the cleansing of our own lives and perspectives in order that we may hear in Joshua's ancient message the literal promise of the Lord.

With the stern personal disciplines implied in this cleansing of our own lives in the background of our thinking, I invite you to join me in a quest for new confidence in the church of Jesus Christ during these days ahead. My ongoing struggle to compose a defensible viewpoint about the church has resulted in the discovery of fresh *hope*—torm-tossed, perhaps, but nonetheless sturdy and vital. It is in this mood and against Joshua's word about tomorrow's wonders that I would speak to all of us now.

A Better Perspective

Florida, like America, is changing dramatically. The beautiful music of evening breezes in the waving palms and the songs of waters from the Atlantic and the Gulf washing over sandy beaches as the tides come in are drowned out by the frightened screams accompanying the persistent infiltration of organized crime and its monstrous cluster of concomitant evils. When the lure of fresh seafood platters is overshadowed by the fear of crack cocaine, the future of our commonwealth is imperiled. Christian men and women know that only the redeeming and restraining influence of the Bible's Holy Faith can be counted upon with confidence to turn back waves of disaster in such situations. The great French agnostic Ernest Renan, writing in 1866 in his classic book *The Apostles*, put it well:

> "Let us enjoy the liberty of the sons of God, but let us take care lest we become accomplices in the diminution of virtues which would menace society if Christianity were to grow weak. What should we do without it?.... If Rationalism wishes to govern the world without regard to the religious needs of the soul, the experience of the French Revolution is there to teach us the consequences of such a blunder."

The plain truth is that history itself teaches us that religion always is necessary to morality. So the church must be strong here in Florida, stronger in the days just ahead than it has ever needed to be in days gone by. Those of us who belong to the Christian community are literally the saviors of civilization, and the trust committed to a savior is one of such import that the ultimate sacrifice may be required. Let us see the task of United Methodism in this burgeoning state as one of supreme and urgent importance, and let us be eager to express our own gratitude for what Florida has meant to us by making the message of Jesus Christ appealing and compelling in this lovely region whose blessings enrich us so much.

There are times when all of us need to move far enough away from the trees to see the wonder of the forest itself. Someone reminded us years ago that we must learn to hear what the centuries have to say to the hours. This is why history's pageantry is always so important if we wish to understand accurately what is happening in the here and now. Florida United Methodism has a noble and thrilling past. I often think of names like P. M. Boyd, Henry W. Blackburn, Ludd Spivey, Charles T. Thrift, Jr., John Hanger, Glenn James, William Ferguson, Mary McLeod Bethune, Howard Berg, Glenn Gold, J. Wallace Hamilton, Clare Cotton, Bishop Angel Fuster, Margaret Hollis Henley, and Violet Hughlett. I knew some of them and wish I could have known them all. That is why I have been so excited over the publication of Robert M. Temple, Jr.'s history of our annual conference entitled *Florida Flame*. Its appearance at this session is a major event and one which all of us who cherish a sacred pride in our task celebrate together. Reading it should make us aware of the endless prayers, labors and sacrifices from which the church in this region has been structured across long years. It should also provide us with fresh perspectives on contemporary problems and opportunities. Thank you, Bob Temple, for work well and faithfully done!

This Is Election Year!

It is an awesome responsibility for an annual conference to have such strong voting power and such wide influence as the Florida Annual Conference possesses. At the 1988 General Conference in St. Louis, United Methodism will be considering momentous issues, including reports from four study commissions (the New Hymnal, the Mission of the church, the Ministry, and Our Theological Task), as well as a large number of critical matters related to policy, polity and program in our great communion. Every General Conference, at least to some extent, rewrites the *Book of Discipline* by which the work of our church is administered. At the 1988 Southeastern Jurisdictional Conference in Lake Junaluska at least five new bishops will be elected, including probably the bishop who will preside over Florida United Methodism for at least two quadrennia. Members of our delegation will be deeply involved in all of these decisions and events.

I plead with you to exercise with thoughtfulness, integrity and prayer the precious franchise which belongs to you as delegates to this session of our annual conference, so that the Holy Spirit, in very fact, may Himself play an influential role in determining the composition of the groups who are to represent us at St. Louis and Lake Junaluska. No more important task confronts us during these particular days together than this one.

The Itinerancy

Twice directly (in 1982 and 1985) and once indirectly (in 1984) I have discussed in my annual address to the Florida Conference the matter of making appointments within the context of the consultative process. I have hoped that my rather extensive dealing with this theme was heard clearly and carefully by members of my cabinet, the preachers of the conference, and the laity. Therefore, what I have to say about the matter this year, I trust, will deal with new material rather than prove to be merely a recapitulation of points made before. If you are interested in reviewing what was said earlier, I refer you to the *Journals* of 1982, 1984 and 1985.

Our church historically deploys its ministers through appointments by the bishop and cabinet annually, and every preacher whose character is passed by the annual conference is guaranteed a pulpit in which to proclaim the gospel, just as every church is guaranteed a minister. I say without equivocation that the task of appointing the preachers in this particular year has been the most difficult such experience I have had in *twenty-two years* of this responsibility. I have been comforted modestly by conversations with other bishops in other parts of the church who have reported similar difficulty.

The consultative process is a new procedure in the life of United Methodism, designed to help appointment-making be more democratic and to increase the probability that the right preacher is sent to a given church. It is far from perfected at this point, and going through its specific steps is an arduous task for the cabinet, the preachers and their families, and pastor-parish committees in local churches. It *never* means that either preachers or churches can make their own appointments, for our "sent" system of deploying ministry cannot function in that way. To be sure, the bishop and cabinet understand that highly individual circumstances exist in many, many cases. They are prepared to exercise great patience and understanding in such instances, and for a large amount of time to be consumed in following the prescribed process. The identification of specific problems in this presentation is not intended in any way to be critical of individuals or churches, but simply to state facts in an effort to nurture a better understanding of what has to be done and some knowledge of the reasons it cannot always be done with ease or visible fairness. Let mention four matters.

1. If a preacher must impose upon the cabinet certain geographical restrictions with relation to his or her assignment, this often means that the cabinet is unable to offer this preacher as good an appointment as otherwise might be true. We saw numerous instances of this during the current appointment-making sessions. But there is an even more serious issue at stake here. Some of our preachers seem unwilling to go into certain districts of our annual conference, even when the situation is attractive and the salary appealing. This is why, upon occasion, a person may appear to have been given a very large advance for no apparent good reason. The appointment which this person is sent to fill may have been turned down by others, and he or she, in the final analysis, was the only satisfactory candidate *willing* to accept the assignment.

2. It has always been true in United Methodism that there are times when preachers must be asked to move before normal tenure in given places has been achieved, and in spite of the fact that their churches have asked for them to return. The reason for this is that particular charges are needed in the appointment-making process to make the system work fairly and equitably. There are numerous such cases this year, and sometimes there is understandable resentment. However, this is one of the prices we pay for the guaranteed appointment system, and it generally can be counted upon to affect the average minister at least once in his or her career. Simply making the system work acceptably calls for a degree of dedication which, if it is ever lost out of the ministry or the churches, will surely doom the appointment-making process as we now know it.

3. In so-called "good" times, and in a conference as large as the Florida

Annual Conference, it is often true that effective ministers can be moved to salary advantages when they are given new appointments. But this *always* depends upon a satisfactory number of openings through retirement or vocational change, and the absence of people returning from special appointments, leaves of absence, sabbaticals, etc. We have had several years in this conference when these circumstances were fortunate, and the habit of salary advance has become part of our professional expectation. This particular year, the circumstances in both instances were quite restrictive and it would not have been possible to make our appointments at all without the willingness on the part of a number of ministers, including two cabinet members, to take substantial reductions in salary in accepting new assignments. This is always a sad development for a conscientious cabinet, since all of us know that health and educational expenses, for example, are very real factors in the fiscal solvency of parsonage families. But we have a year now when relatively few salary advances are possible and *many* salary reductions are occurring in the moving process. We may be sure that somewhere down the road *another* such year will come, and it is wise to build this awareness into our pattern of expectations.

4. Some churches actually decline to accept ministers over 50 years old—and not only deprive themselves of rich service but, in fact, make it literally impossible to do a good job in assigning preachers.

Bishop Roy Hunter Short, sometime episcopal leader of the Florida Conference, in his book entitled *United Methodism in Theory and Practice*, declares that our ministry is *called, educated, mobile, expendable* and *dedicated*. Unless Bishop Short is right, and unless those of us who compose that ministry in this radically different era are able to apply to ourselves anew these classic characteristics of ministry, the undeniable fact is that *the itinerancy as we know it in our church today will not exist by the end of this century*. I have seen the specter of this threat too clearly for comfort this very year!

The Primacy of Stewardship

We have been through a period of years in this conference when we found ourselves wrestling, sometimes in bewilderment, with a gigantic fiscal problem. We were startled to discover, shortly after my own administration began, that a large amount of money raised in a conference-wide campaign for ministerial pensions had not been remitted to the General Board of Pensions in Evanston as required, but had been used instead to help operate Florida United Methodism day-by-day over a period of months and even years. We actually had used pension campaign revenues and other designated monies to make up the difference between what we budgeted annually and what was actually paid by our churches. It was a serious, a tragic situation and required direct and immediate confrontation by all of us. After the conference had been given the facts, the Council on Ministries and other agencies, led by the Council on Finance and Administration and the cabinet, embarked upon a program of intentional austerity augmented by a line item in our annual budget dedicated to the gradual repayment of our debt to ourselves. It has been a difficult road to travel, and many of our leaders have had to forego dreams and plans for a better church and a more exciting adventure in Christian mission in order that we might achieve again *rudimentary fiscal solvency.* As all of us know, there is never much glamour in paying debts—but as all of us also know, debts have to be paid before it is safe to develop new plans and programs. The universal cooperation of our laity and clergy in this vast, unexpected and unprecedented enterprise is paying off gloriously and I am privileged to share good news with all of you who are a part of this annual conference and have sacrificed to achieve a solution to this problem. I hope you will carry these glad tidings home with you and share them with our people who cannot be in Lakeland this week.

1. All Florida Conference pension revenues are now properly in place in our General Church offices in Evanston, as they should be, and while they were estimated to earn *6%* interest, have actually earned *15%* during the past year—and are 1-1/2 years ahead of our best projection for them.
2. Our deficit, on which we have labored so diligently and faithfully these recent years, has been reduced from *$1,600,000* to *$171,643* as of April 30—and should be eliminated entirely on or before December 31 of this year. The Council on Finance and Administration is asking us to continue to budget a line item of $500,000 in order to establish a badly needed but now non-existent reserve fund. Payment of this amount for two years will yield the basic reserve required to enable this conference to operate annually *without having to borrow anything from any source* in the future.
3. The Florida Methodist Foundation (I call your attention to pages 98–99 of your Workbook) has taken giant strides toward liquidity and total self-support.
4. The giving on the part of our churches thus far this fiscal year *is significantly ahead* of the giving last fiscal year.

These are magnificent tidings, and it is you and your churches that have made the effort into a reality. I offer you my personal and official congratulations and gratitude. One of the primary objectives I have had these recent years has been to hand over to my successor on September 1, 1988, a *solvent annual conference.* Through your understanding and help, and by God's grace, this now seems to be a viable hope.

I have harbored a grotesque fear that our disciplined labors to retire our indebtedness might stifle our Kingdom interest and destroy or seriously lessen our vision, our boldness, our spiritual aggressiveness and our faith. Persistent efforts to pay a debt can make a one-time generous person into a miser because of the development of habits of extraordinary caution and austerity. This could become a tragedy for Florida United Methodism, and could prevent our moving with excitement and courage into the 1990s.

Another reality is important. We shall not be able to prevent *the recurrence of fiscal insolvency* until and unless we work assiduously at lifting the level of stewardship in our annual conference. This means a fresh conviction on the part of all of us that God's work requires and deserves more generous financial support than we are giving it now.

I come with two positive proposals tonight. The first is that each of us, clerical and lay, commit or recommit himself or herself to the practice of tithing or proportionate giving, beginning now. Second, I propose that we make an all-out effort throughout our fourteen districts to pay *in full* our total World Service asking and our total Conference Service and Administration Fund for this calendar year.

I quote again those great words of Malachi 3:10: "Bring ye all the tithes into the storehouse, that there may be meat in mine house, and prove me now herewith, saith the Lord of hosts, if I will not open you the windows of heaven and pour you out a blessing, that there shall not be room enough to receive it." I invite you to the greatest joy you have ever known. I invite our churches into the largest freedom they have ever experienced. And I call our great annual conference to the glad and full assumption of its total responsibilities in the Kingdom of our Lord and Savior Jesus Christ.

At the close of this worship service tonight, with the full approval of the Florida Annual Conference's official leadership, I shall join you in a simple act of covenant which, under God, can be the beginning of a new day in our individual lives and in the life of our churches. We are God's stewards, and if we go back to our own congregations and lead them to do likewise, they will become God's stewards also in a way that shall betoken the arrival of a new era in our own community of faith.

Through Lenses of Hope

Bishop Richard B. Wilke calls his book *Are We Yet Alive?* "a scream in the night." It is a scream that helped to awaken a sleeping church, a church buried in its own bureaucratic rationalizations and often forgetting its central purpose while becoming caught up in a plethora of peripheral activities and projects. Now comes the blunt, candid, almost pontifical volume from the pens of two Duke professors, William H. Willimon and Robert L. Wilson, entitled *Rekindling the Flame*, and also Dr. Hinson's *A Place to Dig In*. I agree emphatically with what they seek to do. They are attempting to cause this great church of ours, floundering upon the reefs of its own errors and apparently unable to use effectively its vast powers, to turn around mid-stream and begin a journey toward the beckoning harbor of its divine destiny on whose docks, awaiting its arrival with eager welcome in their eyes, stand people like John Wesley, Francis Asbury, Harry Hosier, Lady Huntingdon—and Jesus of Nazareth. United Methodist people who are willing to examine their own beloved church and to assimilate what many are saying about it and urging it to be and do, are beginning now to view its future through lenses of hope, hope that is Biblical, realistic and honest. In that vivid Old Testament metaphor, there is "the sound of a going in the tops of the mulberry trees."

There are difficulties along the way. The recent scathing article by Henry Fairlie in *The New Republic* entitled "Evangelists in Babylon" is a totally devastating analysis of the fall of the PTL dynasty and the threatened collapse of other empires erected by the electronic evangelists. Fairlie writes these words:

> "The far greater sin of which the big electronic preachers are guilty is the greed on which their satrapies within the empire of televangelism have been built. Both the gospel and example of Christ are used to exploit the poor and the meek (the very people in whose aid the gospel was preached) to create large fortunes; to build mighty pleasure domes greater than Xanadu; to surround preachers with security guards so that their ill-deeds shall not be investigated; to try to intimidate all opposition; to offer high-heeled boots with flowers stuck on them in place of the crucifix; to build a prayer tower when it was enough for Christ to sink to his knees in Gethsemane; to do nothing in the name of Christ unless they are highly paid for it; to offer a version of Christianity, both in preaching and by example, in which there is not a jot or tittle that will recall the lives, say, of St. Francis of Assisi, St. Teresa of Avila, and in our own time, of Mother Teresa of Calcutta, is a sinning almost beyond the imagination."

Fairlie might have added that this kind of sinning is not necessarily peculiar to the big televangelists about whom we have heard and read so much in recent weeks. Even in our own church there could come revelations of mis-doing which, for some, will shake the foundations of faith. This is true in other great churches as well. Why? Because we are all human, subject to temptation, creatures of fragile dust, and the only hope we have is in the death and resurrection of a Savior. But the church is of God and came down from Him out of Heaven. This we must always remember, and the wonder of wonders is that God can use frail human beings, who periodically make their pilgrimages to Babylon, to accomplish His tasks here upon earth. The only greater wonder is that He can look upon our sins, even ours, and when we repent, place them under the blood of Jesus Christ and so remove them from us as far as the east is removed from the west! Praise His holy name!

But even these difficulties, these tragic detours which both tempt and threaten the pilgrim people of God as they seek to quicken their steps along the highway that leads to a new day for the church, do not destroy the glorious fact that a slumbering giant is awakening and that our own great United Methodism has heard, as it were, a scream in the night and is seeking to find ways of response. We are beginning to look again through lenses of hope, and this means some very practical things. First of all, it means that we must address the problem within our own lives and congregations. Too often we have been eager to offer our cynical criticisms of the organized church *at large*. Too often we have failed to address these problems *where we are*.

Dare I tell you a ridiculous story to illustrate this point? It is about a town in which there was a doughnut road. It all began when one doughnut manufacturer opened his shop and placed outside it a sign which said "The Best Doughnuts in Town." A little later another shop opened with the sign "The Best Doughnuts in the State." A third competitor appeared and installed a marquee with this lettering: "The Best Doughnuts in the Country." Soon a fourth store opened, advertising that it sold "The Best Doughnuts in the World." Finally an enterprising doughnut manufacturer came to town, surveyed the scene, rented a place at the end of the same avenue, opened his business and installed a sign which said simply "The Best Doughnuts on This Street!" The ultimate efficacy of all our Kingdom efforts is expressed in what happens not somewhere else in the country or the world, but in that little corner of God's garden over which we and we alone have been given precious stewardship. Our task in rich old East Tennessee jargon is "to deliver our own precinct!" *That's all—but it's enough*. Of course, it is all founded on what we really *believe, intend* and *practice* about God and His son Jesus Christ, our Lord and Savior. Behind the work of the cabinet, the staff, district councils and committees, local church boards and groups, there are always and inevitably the creed and commitment of every preacher and lay person. When Joshua long ago declared to all the children of Israel as they sought to advance behind the Ark of the Covenant into the Land of Promise, "tomorrow the Lord will do wonders among you," he prefaced his bold assertion of trust and hope with the stipulation that those who heard him, if they were to enter into such a magnificent miracle, must *first* have prepared themselves. The message is the same today, as this new session of our conference begins: God's Word is sure, but whether its wonders will take place here must depend in the end upon you and me.

We must really believe God. While I was bishop of the Charlotte Area, in the turbulent days of the 1960s when I had led my conference in racial integration and appointed the first Black superintendent in the Southeastern Jurisdiction to the Winston-Salem district, my life had been threatened time and time again and I had employed with my own money someone to stay in our house with my wife and our young son during the many occasions when I had to be away from home in my work. I recall one Sunday when I preached in a large country church near Concord, North Carolina, not far from the center of one segment of the vast Ku Klux Klan organization in that state. My subject was the love of God. After the sermon, a big burly giant of a man in shirt sleeves, collar open and without a necktie, ruddy-faced, the tendons in his neck standing out like rods of steel, his eyes flashing with excitement, the traditional image of a recalcitrant red-neck in those chaotic days, came sauntering down the aisle to where I stood greeting the people. He pushed through the crowd, took hold of my coat lapels and literally glared into my face. Then he spoke. "Buddy," he said, "do you believe that a man can live what you have been preaching this morning and still belong to the Klan?" I thought my time had come. I looked at him for a moment and then answered, perhaps more softly than was my habit, "No, sir, I do not." He replied, "I don't either, and tomorrow morning I'm getting out of the Klan!" God's Spirit had converted him – and saved me! But I had to *believe* God, and perhaps to risk my life on that belief.

We must really mean it. Our religion and what we do about it must matter to us more than anything else in life. When we lived in Nashville, we heard much about, and often saw, Tom T. Hall. My eccentric Southern Baptist friend of many years, Will Campbell, in his wonderful memoir entitled *Forty Acres and a Goat* tells of the time when Hall, at the close of the Democratic Convention in Miami Beach in 1972, heard an old caretaker mumbling as he cleaned up the convention debris words which Tom T. Hall wrote into a country song that became a classic:

> "There ain't but three things in this world
> That's worth a solitary dime;
> That's old dogs, and children,
> And watermelon wine."

When I read Will's recollection of this event, I remembered Irving Bacheller's great novel *Eben Holden* where he makes his principal character say something similar, yet very, very different:

> "When everything else in life is gone,
> All that's left will be God and love and Heaven!"

Which is it for you and me? On what are we staking our lives? Is it the equivalent of old dogs, little children and watermelon wine? Or is it God and love and Heaven, the teachings of the Holy Bible, the truth of the Christian faith, the wonder of the message of our own United Methodism? *Do we really mean it?* If so, we can read the headlines about Jim and Tammy Bakker and others like them, even news about an occasional United Methodist leader whose humanness seems to triumph over his commitment, and not really be swayed. When I was in Nashville for Holy Week services a month ago, I read Jerry Thompson's column in *The Tennessean*, entitled "Thompson's Station." It dealt with the PTL fiasco and all of its attendant events, deploring the whole scandalous panorama. Then it closed with this unforgettable paragraph:

> "When I go to church, it's at Martin's Chapel United Methodist in
> Robertson County. And when I drop something in the collection plate,
> I know it will be put to good use. It'll also be fully accounted for. And
> if there is a sickness in the family, a death or someone needs counseling
> or comforting, Brother Marvin Champion will be there. The next time
> you need a preacher, try calling Jim, Jimmy, Oral, or Jerry and see how
> quickly they come. Better yet, just try getting any one of them on the
> phone. If you do, ask them where the money really goes."

Do we mean it? Is our faith mature enough to be unshakeable in times of crisis, and never to waver from our primary commitment to do the Lord God's will here upon earth and to strengthen His church that it may go on doing His work long after we are gone?

We must really practice it all. Carlyle Marney, my friend for long years, used to say the word "church" is a verb! What he meant was that no confession of faith, no mere sermon or testimony is a substitute for action. Bill Hinson, in his new book, tells about how George Whitefield used to say in a sermon, "I will go to prison for you and I will go to death with you, but I won't go to Heaven without you." When this kind of passion begins to characterize the pastors and lay people of this annual conference, God's events will begin to happen. We have here in Florida a faithful and effective minister who signs his message to his parishioners every week with the statement "The Shepherd Loves the Sheep." Life is never passive, always active!

William James, the great Harvard psychologist, used to say that religion is either like a dull habit or an acute fever.

Dear friends, our basic problem as we look at the things we ought to do in stewardship, in evangelism, in mission is not financial, nor academic, nor even theological. It is *motivational!* We can lead our people into a great awakening of stewardship, of the practice of tithing and proportionate giving, of enthusiastic support for those great ecclesiastical and Kingdom causes that command our allegiance, provided there is enough fire in the bones of those who are here this week to cause the flames to begin in the people back home when we return to our congregations! If we are to see the future of our beloved church and the future of Florida itself through lenses of hope, then we must be willing to pay the price of *sanctifying ourselves*, to return to Joshua's great words, so that tomorrow the Lord will do wonders among us!

Not long ago, in the city of Washington, DC, I participated in an evening's program more thrilling and inspiring than most of those I can recall in my entire ministry. The speakers were the Honorable John Brademas, former United States Representative from the State of Indiana and Majority Whip of the House of Representatives, now President of New York University, and the Honorable Harry A. Blackmun, Associate Justice of the United States Supreme Court, both deeply dedicated United Methodist lay people. The burden of their two addresses, each of which was brilliantly sensitive to the complex and dangerous nuances of today's world situation, was that the church of Jesus Christ is the only viable hope human society has as it rushes toward century's end. Each of these great Americans in his own way brought a vast audience of 2,000 United Methodist people and clergy to a fresh crescendo of confidence in God and assurance that He "will do wonders among us" even yet! There was the breath of resurrection, the faint but lovely light of new morning, the trumpet of victory in the midst of battle's terror and agony. *God would prevail!*

This, as Joshua first reminded us long, long ago, is our sure and shining hope! My earnest prayer is for Heaven's cleansing in our souls, for deliverance from the shackling chains of pettiness and our narrow, negative perspectives, and for a fresh grasp in our hearts and minds upon all the dear promises of God. In the spirit of such a prayer and as your chief pastor, I admonish you in Merrill's stirring words:

> "Rise up, O Saints of God,
> Have done with lesser things;
> Give heart and mind and soul and strength
> To serve the King of kings!"

Amen and Amen!

XI

Methodists in the North Europe Central Conference, Vasteras, Sweden, 1972

This is an address given at the North Europe Central Conference in Vasteras, Sweden, in the summer of 1972. The message was offered through an interpreter and was, therefore, necessarily rather brief. Bishop Ole E. Borgen was presiding over the Conference the evening that I spoke. I have a vivid recollection of the fluent exchanges of conversation in more than one of the Scandinavian languages, but especially do I recall the very frequent use of the word "tak"—which means "thank you" in Norwegian.

The Conference was composed of the unusually intelligent clerical delegates who seem always to lead our church in its European expressions, and of an almost surprisingly large number of distinguished lay delegates. I remember a certain internationally known physician who was with us for the entire period of the Conference.

I elected to speak on the basic Christological doctrines of our religion and this seemed to be well received, perhaps better than it would have been in the United States.

Always one comes away from such a gathering deeply impressed with the highly visible evidences of persistent dedication and a sure conviction of Christian identity that seem to characterize those who have maintained their faith through great hardship.

Methodists in the North Europe Central Conference, Vasteras, Sweden, 1972

Bishop Borgen, other bishops, my dear Christian friends:

Mrs. Hunt and I come not only to bring you cordial greetings from the Council of Bishops of our great church, but also to offer the deep gratitude of our own souls to this important and far-flung portion of World Methodism. We have visited briefly in the beautiful Scandinavian territory before, and have known the powerful yet gentle Christian witness of Bishop and Mrs. Odd Hagen and the eager, energetic evangelical leadership of Bishop and Mrs. Ole Borgen. Bishop Borgen was educated in my own episcopal Area in the United States, and is greatly beloved there. We have read the exciting history of "The Bethel Ship" with O. G. Hedström, Ole Peterson, Boie Smith, John Peter Larsson and two Swedish-speaking Finnish brothers who brought the Methodist interpretation of the gospel to the Nordic world. We have traveled throughout the land of Bishop Sommer and Bishop Wunderlich, and heard the stories of Christoph Müller, Ludwig Jacoby and John L. Nuelson. We have enjoyed the hospitality of Bishop Härtel in East Berlin and have toured the great Pergamon Museum with him. We know firsthand about the amazing spiritual vigor of Methodism in the German nation. We have seen the labors of faithful Christian leaders like the Nausners and Willie Reyser in Bishop Schaefer's Austrian Methodism, building on foundations laid long ago by Baroness Von Langenau, Otto Melle, our dear friend Bishop Ferdinand Sigg and others. We know, in some measure at least, the indebtedness of World Methodism to the Northern Europe Central Conference churches and people for *accurate understanding of the Christian gospel* in a day of confusion and apostasy and for *faithful pursuit of the church's fundamental mission* in our troubled world. And so, our greeting is one of strong and warm Christian love, reaching across the waters and over the miles, and also one of genuine appreciation and thanksgiving. We are honored to be in your midst and are grateful for your kindnesses to us.

Let me speak briefly against the backdrop of II Corinthians 5:19: "God was in Christ reconciling the world unto himself." This text speaks of the centrality of that Strange Man who, as an American essayist put it years ago, has ploughed his way into the experience of the world. He and his mighty victory are the themes of New Testament Christianity, the roots of our religion. The tragic impoverishment of the church's witness in recent years is traceable to the persistent ignoring, often in high places, of the naked spiritual power implicit in a full awareness of God's work through Jesus Christ in his Incarnation, his death on the Cross, and his Resurrection. I propose that only in our re-discovery of these three imperishable acts of God shall we see the renewal of the church in our time.

The Incarnation

The Incarnation. "God was in Christ..." (II Corinthians 5:19). How incongruous this assertion has seemed in recent years! One of the surprisingly prominent illusions of our era is that God is *absent* from his creation. An American theologian, Professor William Hamilton, has said: "We are not talking about the absence of the experience of God, but about the experience of the absence of God." Bonhoeffer spoke about God "allowing himself to be edged out of the world." The beginnings of this view are complex. Certainly it is an effort to interpret in terms of faith a weird age of the world's history. It undertakes to account for secularism's triumph. Fearing that the older theistic and theological views of life and history cannot survive contemporary revolutions, it seeks to make a new and radically different road: it is secular theology, religionless Christianity. Most of all, this illusion of illusions is based upon man's arrogant metaphysical and actual independence of God. *It rests upon the assumption that modern man can get along very well indeed without God.*

What an illusion! A man prays and knows an answer. A dying soldier is told of the love of God that will not let him go, and peace and hope shine in his eyes. A great congregation sings with enthusiasm "A mighty fortress is our God" and the atmosphere of worship is charged with living power. A man who has just learned that he has inoperable cancer receives Holy Communion and rises with quiet courage to take up his tasks for the time that remains. A member of some great national Parliament talks frankly with his pastor and then goes to vote his Christian conviction on some important issue, aware that the deed may cost him an election. A student kneels to pray at night, taunted by some of those with whom he lives. *God absent from his creation?* What an illusion!

Or take yourself—you who do not always believe in him, who think you operate your life with reasonable efficiency and effectiveness without him. Can you be honest enough to recall a moment when some alluring temptation to dishonor brought your soul to the edge of a precipice—and *Something* held you back? Can you in candor remember an hour dark with human need when suddenly light and help appeared? Or what about a memory that rose at nighttime to rebuke you or to bless you? Or a great and ennobling thought that broke unexpectedly across the barren terrain of your mind? Or some strange and exhilarating exultation after you had seen a great play or read a memorable book? Or the warm glow somewhere within you as you shared intimate fellowship with a dear and trusted friend? Or the sorrow of some bereavement? Or the ecstatic gladness of a beautiful surprise? *God absent from his creation?* What an illusion!

The Incarnation, foundational doctrine of the Christian religion, reminds us again and afresh that God is forever present with us in his creation. He is not absent from his creation. This is history's supreme fact, and its message of nearly incredible hope and joy is a light for life's dark valleys and a song in its long nights. The God who made us has come to save us!

The Crucifixion

The Crucifixion. The Cross, for me at least, is not ultimately subject to minute theological analysis. Men and women have seen many ideas in it: sacrifice, atonement, ransom, substitution—each with at least a portion of truth to contribute to the whole. The Cross is vastly bigger than the ideas men and women have had about it. It looks down, with understanding, upon Grotius and Anselm and Abelard and all the others who have sought to reduce it to theories. Emil Brunner came as close as words may approach when he declared that we see three realities on Calvary: "The inviolable holiness of God; the absolute impossibility of overlooking human sin; and the illimitable mercy of God."

Years ago a Methodist layman gave me a copy of *Christ and His Cross* by the English lay theologian, William Russell Maltby. In this book is a hauntingly beautiful story about a workingman in the North of England whose wife, soon after her marriage, drifted into vicious ways and went rapidly from bad to worse. He came home one Sunday evening to find, as he had found a dozen times before, that she had gone on a new debauch. He knew in what condition she would return, after two or three days of a nameless life. He sat down in the cheerless house to look the truth in the face and to determine what he must do. The worst had happened too often to leave him much hope of amendment, and he saw at least in part what might be in store for him. He made his choice to hold by his wife to the end and to keep a home for her who would not make one for him. Now that a new and terrible meaning had passed into the words "for better, for worse" he re-affirmed his marriage vow. Later, when someone who knew them both intimately ventured to remonstrate with him, he answered: "Not a word! She is my wife! I loved her when she was a girl in our village, and I shall love her as long as there is breath in my body." She did not mend, and died in his house after some years, in a shameful condition, with his hands spread over her in pity and prayer to the last. Surely this was love to the uttermost! And surely this is the power of the Cross.

This is our message—not cleverness of human thought—but Jesus Christ and him crucified: forgiveness of sin, redemption for lost and lonely humankind!

The Resurrection

The Resurrection. The Resurrection is the final, necessary clause of the sentence whose earlier parts have dealt with the Incarnation and the Crucifixion—the *crescendo* of Christ's mighty victory. If the identity of Jesus Christ is our authority for the Christian enterprise and the redemption of the Cross our message, then the Resurrection is our hope and the earnest of our triumph. My dear friend Dr. James S. Stewart of Edinburgh has said, "There had now appeared, in the midst of time, life in a new dimension.... The early Christians were not merely preaching the Resurrection as a fact; they were living in it as in a new country."

In one of my pastorates there was a lovely and radiant young woman upon whose life heavy sufferings converged. Her husband was an alcoholic whose tragic condition defied the corrective efforts of successive ministers and a regiment of friends, and made him insensitive to the claims of responsibility, honor and love. Debts rocketed, community derision for the man she loved cut her to the quick, financial duress kept her working though physically ill and decreed that she must not use her earnings for herself. But there was something memorably buoyant about her. She never lost hope, others did for her, but not she. The commonest kindness, the tiniest scrap of good news became a harbinger of better things ahead in her perennially confident heart. Each new morning was a magic scroll, a parchment of reverent optimism. Life was new and something marvelous might happen before nightfall! One day I had preached on "The Christian Hope" and her eyes danced in excitement as she thanked me for letting her hear a fresh utterance of the message God had given to her long before! She died—all too soon, we thought—but with the banners of ecstatic expectancy flying yet over a debris of terrible heartaches. She was our lady of the Resurrection Hope.[1]

Today's headlines and telecasts have little of a hopeful nature to suggest about the coming of the Kingdom of God! Continuing ideological struggles; the diabolically mad nuclear armament race; the devastating revolution in morals—crime, sex perversion, drugs, alcohol; the generation gap; the lingering, senseless terror of the war in Vietnam; mind and behavior manipulation; genetic engineering; the ethical implications of organ transplants; racism of all colors; violence; lawlessness—and so it goes. But in the midst of all of this and in spite of all of it—the perceptive Christian glimpses a strange and wonderful *wistfulness* about our tragic moment in history. He senses with tremulous hope that the long tide is turning.

This is the pledge of the Resurrection for our century. And so hope surges again within us, moral muscles tighten, spiritual vision clears, and fear's palpitations know a great calm.

Conclusion

Religion is not just philosophy. When the human mind begins to develop its clever dialectics of God and man, sin and redemption, death and life, it is not necessarily dealing with the gospel. Sermons, even sermons, can prove to be exciting intellectual encounters with fascinating ideas, even ideas about the Bible, lofty philosophical monologues in which the holy, transforming presence of the living, loving, compassionate Lord is totally missing. There is no burning bush, no cry from Calvary, and there are rarely changed lives in the wake of such preaching. The gospel is not a dialectic of logic, not a system of ethics, not a musty set of morals, not a book of platitudes. The gospel is love's aching arms when life is lonely and barren. The gospel is inconceivable forgiveness when sin has been bleak and persistent. The gospel is hope when hope is long gone, dawning's bright fingers clutching at the throat of night. The gospel is life when death has done its hideous worst. The gospel is the everlasting light of Christ's mighty victory in the Incarnation, on the Cross and in the Resurrection. This—and only this—is the foundation for our message about both personal and social religion. "God was in Christ reconciling the world unto himself."

You who are the Methodist Christians of Europe have helped the rest of us around the world to recall the centrality of this great and fundamental gospel. We are your brothers and sisters forever because of your emphasis. And now may the power of this mighty message sustain you and all of your churches in the great tasks which you confront following this Central Conference.

Et semper Deus tecum sit!

Endnotes

[1] *Recovering the Sacred*, Earl G. Hunt, Jr., Lake Junaluska, NC: The Jonathan Creek Press, 1992, pages 150–151.

XII

The United Methodist Church and Its Relationship to Its Academic Institutions

This is a major study document, the last I have produced. It was done at the direction of the Teaching Concerns Committee of the Council of Bishops. It was a feature of the November session of the Council in 1998, held at Epworth-By-The-Sea, Georgia.

Bishop James Thomas moved its passing by the Teaching Concerns Committee, and with minimal discussion the response, as far as I could tell, was unanimously affirmative. The next day it was brought to the Council plenary session as a part of the Teaching Concerns report. I detected no negative votes when this report was approved.

The study document was then sent officially to Dr. Ken Yamada at the Board of Higher Education and Ministry in Nashville. He was familiar with much of its content during the process of writing. I have always been perplexed about what really happened to the study report which was intended for use with the presidents of our educational institutions. If it ever came to the point of usefulness that had been contemplated for it, I simply am not aware of this fact.

When I debated its inclusion in this publication of papers, it occurred to me that my philosophy concerning the church and higher education could be dated. I sent the document to Dr. Tom Trotter, whose historical and contemporary perspectives on the subject I trust totally. In our subsequent conversation by telephone he made no suggestions or any change and said definitely that he thought the study should be a part of this volume.

The United Methodist Church and Its Relationship to Its Academic Institutions

---

Prologue

The purpose of this paper is to examine both the historic and the contemporary relationship between The United Methodist Church and its academic institutions, particularly its colleges and universities; and to propose guidelines for strengthening this relationship through the involvement of the Council of Bishops. Its hypothesis is simple and unapologetic: the sanctuary needs the academy, and the academy needs the sanctuary. These needs are greater today than they have ever been before.

The sanctuary and the academy, in church-related institutional life, are both gloriously alike and radically different. They share a common passion for truth and a mutual conviction that such truth is grounded in the timeless message of the Judeo-Christian religion. But the sanctuary must grant the academy freedom to be itself and to expound the disciplines that both seek and contain that truth, controlled only by the strictures that guard its own integrity.

Ours is a prodigal world plunged into what is actually both a post-Christian and a post-modern era. It has developed and enthroned an agnostic mind no longer sensitive to the moral parameters that have defined the civilized life for centuries. We must discover how, in this vastly different moment of earth's history, to recapture those values of intellect and soul that make human life compatible with the Divine design. To fail is to invite disaster for our age.

Our church, at its best, has always believed in the unity of faith and learning, and this is why it has built and supported schools. Dean Lynn Harold Hough of Drew University reminded us half a century ago that "true evangelicalism is intelligence on fire."

We possess an incredible treasure in those colleges and universities that acknowledge kinship with the Body of Christ. Many of these now have both administrators and faculty members who are grimly and sensitively aware of today's *amoral* culture and are becoming humbly eager to use their positions to effect substantive changes in our society before it is too late. They need leadership, and this paper will propose that the bishops of our church, in partnership with appropriate church-related educational bodies, consider becoming their leaders. This would be an educational mission, but it would be, in the broadest sense, an evangelistic task as well—a kind of evangelism far removed from sawdust trails, altar calls, inquiry rooms, and the old litanies of revival. It would be a gigantic struggle to bring the human mind into the presence of God, using academe's finely-honed tools, to restore inner commitment to values that are timeless, and to let loose in the world generations of youth who have begun to know again what is required to be fully human and to believe in the vision of the Judeo-Christian tradition.

A Historical Note

That there is a significant reciprocal responsibility existing between many branches of the Christian church and higher education is a condition growing out of the simple fact that education itself in modern times is largely a product of the direct and indirect influences of the church. In seasons of colorful academic gowns and hoods we may well recall that these were originally the costumes of learned monks. Perhaps no movement in the last five hundred years has given quite the impetus to education that came from the Protestant Reformation.

The origin of certain celebrated American colleges and universities further reinforces this fact. In the little village of Bradford, Connecticut, ten ministers of the gospel each set a few books on a table; this was the beginning of what is now Yale University. Harvard, Dartmouth and Amherst were all children of the Congregationalists. William and Mary in Virginia and Columbia in New York were progeny of the Anglicans or Episcopalians. The list could be extended. By 1860 the churches of America had established 179 permanent colleges; and even the 28 state or municipal institutions existing at that time were almost all headed by Christian ministers.

It is no wonder that Alexis de Tocqueville, the French historian, surveying life in America, wrote these words in the early nineteenth century: "In the United States the influence of religion is not confined to the manners, but extends to the intelligence of the people."[1]

The record of The United Methodist Church is remarkable in this arena of Christian mission. From the founding of ill-fated Cokesbury College in 1784, American Methodism implemented aggressively the early dreams of Bishops Asbury and Coke to give the Wesleyan expression of religion on this continent a sound educational foundation. Stellar institutional names like Randolph Macon in Virginia (1830), Wesleyan University in Connecticut (1831), Dickinson in Pennsylvania (1834), Emory College in Georgia (1836), Emory & Henry College in Virginia (1836), and Wesleyan College in Georgia (1836) began to appear. Others were started but did not survive. By the beginning of the Civil War Methodism, according to a recent study by Dr. Russell Richey of Duke University,[2] had succeeded in founding 34 "permanent" colleges. The process continued and at times was accelerated during the following decades. Today, in the United States, many of the academically strong schools in the private sector have relationships of varying closeness to The United Methodist Church, although it must be noted that there has also been some conspicuous attrition, as in the cases of Vanderbilt, Wesleyan University, Northwestern, and the University of Southern California. At the time these words are being written, we have 123 schools, colleges, universities, professional schools and seminaries operating under the auspices of our denomination in this country, and there are 487 additional institutions in the Methodist global network. No other religious communion except Roman Catholicism can approach this record.

While the dialogue sessions for which this paper seeks to prepare will involve only schools located in our five geographical Jurisdictions, it should be stated clearly that our church, from the beginning, has seen its educational mission as being global. Unfortunately, treatment of the many superb institutions related to United Methodism in lands other than the United States will require a separate study—a matter that should be addressed, along with a special inquiry targeting the excellent seminaries of The United Methodist Church.

One bishop, experienced in education, suggests that United Methodist colleges and universities in existence today are in "multiform" relation to the church. He identifies five types of relationships:

1. *Ownership*. Following the Methodist Episcopal Church, South's loss of Vanderbilt University in 1914, two new universities (Emory and Southern Methodist University) were founded with ties of charter and governance so close to the church that the term "ownership," while rarely used or acknowledged by the institutions, is not inaccurate from a practical standpoint.

2. *Trustee Election or Approval*. Certain institutions are related to our church through provision in their charters for the election of some or all of their trustees by an annual conference or annual conferences, or by the General Board of Higher Education and Ministry, or the General Board of Global Ministries. Other institutions, while not requiring actual election, call for approval of election by annual conferences or appropriate general agencies. By actual count, 99 of our schools provide that either a particular annual conference or annual conferences or a designated general agency of The United Methodist Church must participate in either the election or the approval of some or all trustees. The number was 100 until the discontinuance of Sue Bennett College in Kentucky. Of added interest is the fact that 36 of our schools provide that property titles and in some cases net assets, in the event of dissolution or departure from charter provisions,

shall revert to whatever segment of our church is named in the original relationship.

3. *General and Annual Conference Financial Support*. Some institutions are regarded as being so essential to the life and development of the church that the General Conference has placed them in its budget for "designated and significant" funding: the 13 theological schools, the 11 Black Colleges, and Africa University. Many of our colleges are the recipients of financial support on varying levels from the annual conferences to which they relate.

4. *Intentional Association*. An elect group of colleges and universities, some strong enough not to "need" church affiliation, have chosen to remain vitally related to annual conferences, Jurisdictional conferences and even the General Conference. They proudly identify with United Methodism through the presence and activities of their presidents, the employment of competent and church-related faculty members, the inclusion of appropriate religion-oriented courses in their curricula, and through helpful involvement in regional churches. There are some who would suggest that this roll of honor presently is showing hopeful growth.

5. *History*. While they cannot be classified any longer as church-related because of their own initiative in dissolving this association, some very prominent institutions have the stamp of our denomination and its convictions indelibly impressed upon their history, and the church's influence is a permanent part of their character and mystique. Examples would be Vanderbilt University, Wesleyan University, Northwestern University and the University of Southern California.

The Diminishing of a Relationship

It would be an overstatement to declare that the relationship between the church and its institutions of higher learning has been destroyed. However, responsible commentators from both sectors are aware that it appears to be threatened seriously by a number of developments. Among these are the following:

1. There has been, in the past four or five decades, a deliberate effort on the part of some institutions to distance themselves from their supporting ecclesiastical communities. Sometimes the reason has been to avoid legal entanglements, sometimes to prevent real or imagined interference with academic freedom or excellence. Occasionally the action has resulted from an anti-religious bias on the part of either the administration or the faculty, or both.

2. There has been, on the other hand, a willingness among some church

leaders to see the ties between the academy and the sanctuary either weakened or severed. Several rationales have supported this position: an honest conviction that education is better marketed either by the state or by the great independent institutions; a failure to grasp that religious values or insights are an integral part of the kind of higher learning that has as its purpose the improvement of human life; a desire to free the church from any obligation to place its dollars in college or university coffers; and the deliberate prioritizing of other kingdom interests so that higher education, often unintentionally, is either excluded or relegated to a lower level of importance. This perspective surfaced prominently in the General Conference of 1968 (but for a different and essentially a legal reason) when a resolution was passed urging our colleges to consider the abandonment of all church connections—an action based on what later proved to be a misunderstanding of the separation clause in the Constitution's First Amendment.[3]

3. Some of our church institutions, unfortunately, have chosen presidents and/or trustees who have lacked a deep appreciation for the Christian faith, and have assumed either a negative or a neutral view of church-relatedness. This error of judgment has had repercussions in faculty selection, campus policy and institutional climate. It was the late chancellor of Syracuse University, Dr. William P. Tolley, who reminded us years ago that the heart of church relationship is in the college presidency and the trustees.

4. Some annual conferences have failed to supply respectable financial support to their own institutions of higher education, according this cause a conspicuous lack of priority that has resulted in puzzled dismay among the administrations and faculties of these schools and a consequent breakdown of cordiality between the academy and the sanctuary.

5. In rare instances, the church—sometimes with good intentions—has prostituted the educational concept by demanding that its colleges and universities be little more than extended Sunday Schools. A frequent corollary of this error has been an insistence upon improper control of the campus and the classroom, and a resulting resistance on the part of faculty members to the church's intrusion.

Proper Prerogatives and Their Possible Details

Religion at its best and education at its best have always been closely related, a fact noted as long ago as the writings of Anselm and Augustine. Each has recognized the integrity and importance of the other. This has meant *for the church* a willingness to grant the academy certain appropriate prerogatives that ensure its necessary freedom. They include the right of an institution to define its educational mission, design its curriculum, choose its faculty, and guarantee properly qualified teachers the liberty to interpret subject matter in accordance with their best knowledge and understanding. It is this principle of academic freedom that becomes a sentinel safeguarding the whole process of truth seeking which is at the heart of educational motivation. This basic guideline requires that the exercise of academic freedom by an institution must be accomplished *always* within a context of *total responsibleness*.

Another duty of the church to its colleges or universities involves both moral and financial support. The former is as essential as the latter, and both are inescapable obligations of a church that wishes to be characterized as "*college-related*." Unquestionably, the accomplishment of such dual support requires the close partnership of bishops and institutional heads.

Finally, and of supreme significance, the church needs to help recruit United Methodist students for its schools. It is good that young persons from other denominations and those with no religious affiliation are welcome in our institutions. However, if our large investment of interest, concern and dollars is to produce proper dividends, our splendid college offerings must attract the attention and elicit the response of *many more* United Methodist youth—an essential task that falls back primarily upon the local church and its pastoral leadership, but that can be encouraged effectively by the bishop. Implicit in this undertaking may be the challenge to provide scholarship help to offset escalating educational costs.

On the other hand, mutual recognition of the integrity and importance of the other has meant *for the school* an intentional acceptance and cultivation of the fundamental values and principles of the Christian religion, and readiness to work sincerely and constantly within a correct collegial relationship with the church. Certain specifics may be mentioned:

A church-related college, or a university on its undergraduate level, should accept the obligation to seek at least a conspicuous coterie of Christian scholars for its faculty, in order to expose a student generation to a visible Christian witness. It is important that those within such a coterie should be individuals of strong intellectual capacity, outstanding academic credentials and excellent potential as classroom teachers. The reason for this is obvious: those faculty members primarily responsible for presenting a Christian witness must be able to command authentic campus respect.

1. Such an institution should include in its curriculum certain basic and attractive courses designed to acquaint students with the fundamentals of Biblical knowledge, the meanings of the Christian faith, and the influence

of Christianity in history. As a rule, these courses should be elective, since it is never the proper role of the church-related institution to enforce attention or response to the Christian message, but rather to provide exposure to it in a manner consonant with good scholarship and academic decorum.

2. Thankfully, some students who matriculate in college are already religiously committed and motivated, while others reach such a status during their college careers. The church-related college must keep as one of its central purposes the graduation of young persons who are well-prepared to serve and lead in local United Methodist churches in the communities where they will eventually establish residences. This requires persistent skill on the part of the college in supplying through course content and in other ways a basic knowledge of our denomination's history, structure and polity, and in helping students develop an informed appreciation of the institutional church and a compassionate awareness of its problems. Too, the church-related college must engage in the timely and steady nurture of those students who are in the process of preparing for seminary and/or full-time Christian service. Both of these ministries of cultivation by its schools constitute extremely important services to the church.

3. The institution of the church should seek to bring on campus each school year a number of distinguished and well-known Christian leaders for chapel and lyceum programs, and to give guest classroom lectures or, in some instances, to serve as visiting professors for a term. One bishop, himself a former president of a church-related college, alluded to the "process of gentle spiritual osmosis" which can captivate young people when they "rub shoulders with God's giants."

4. The institution should seek ways to be helpful to the annual conference and regional churches, using both students and faculty in acts of reciprocation for church support, and in order to facilitate contact for the students with religious leadership and local congregations as a vital part of their educational experience. A college choir would be one example of an appropriate vehicle through which this kind of contact may be achieved.

5. It is important for the church-related institution to have the effective ministry of a campus chaplain. The individual chosen for this task should be an attractive, committed Christian with a positive attitude toward the church, a natural affinity for youth, and an empathetic understanding of the complex and formidable problems associated with being young in today's world. In order to earn proper campus prestige, it may be helpful for this staff member either to possess or to acquire the necessary credentials for faculty status.

The costs of bringing Christian dignitaries to campus, (4) above, and of maintaining the office of chaplain, (6) above, will require substantial funding. A possible source of such funding would be an allocation from the church's annual financial gift to the institution—an arrangement which, when made known to the church, could prove to be rich in public relations possibilities.

In all aspects of a school's relationship to the church, including the foregoing six points, a significant caveat applies: the office of religion is that of influence and counsel where the educational process is concerned, and never control. The climate to be sought is one of trust and warmth, a goal that can be achieved best through deliberate episcopal and presidential collaboration.

The Need for Church-Related Institutions

Education and religion need each other. The school needs the church and the church needs the school. In the realm of knowledge, as one thoughtful member of the Council of Bishops has put it, "the *how* of science and technology has surpassed the *why* of philosophy and theology." The incredulities of bio-physics have so captivated the human brain that little thought is being devoted to an understanding of life's ultimate meaning, its purposes and goals, and its necessary prohibitions. As an example, we are ill-prepared to offer a convincing ethical evaluation of the scientific processes that can now produce radical alterations of life forms and one day may be ready to attempt the cloning of human beings.

The ancient query of the Psalmist, "What are human beings that you are mindful of them, mortals that you care for them?" (Psalm 8:4), baffles the contemporary person. A true definition of education demands theological input, particularly teleological and eschatological insights, if the deep, rich meanings of Divine design and ultimate objectives are to be grasped. Otherwise, the educational process, to quote the same bishop again, can only result in "improved means to unimproved ends," and may well harbor the seeds of apocalyptic disaster. Only the church-related college with its unique capacity to introduce the spiritual perspectives of the Christian faith into the quest for knowledge can be counted upon to develop with any certainty the kind of leadership needed to build communities of hospitality and irenic camaraderie instead of hatred and violence.

Today's student will enter upon a world of startling religious and racial diversity whose population growth is outdistancing the earth's resources. It is a world with a devastatingly competitive global economy, and a scientific genius with no moral compass to govern it. It is a planet where nuclear and biological weapons exist and are in the possession not only of the so-called superpowers but also, and even especially, of certain unpredictable and irresponsible rogue nations that are not actually a part of the world community. Sometimes this student is unrelated to the church, poorly grounded in academic fundamentals, already exposed and perhaps addicted to drugs, alcohol and sexual liberty, and has no clear comprehension of what is sacred. Such a student needs the educational experience to produce for him or her a positive and life-changing metamorphosis. On the other hand, if a student is already committed to a serious and constructive view of life, then the educational experience needs to offer guidance and encouragement in navigating the treacherous waters of present-day existence.

The current secularization of life has robbed society of much of its God-consciousness and its hard-earned sensitivity to moral and spiritual values. The classical approach to knowledge through intense exposure to the great books and ideas of the ages has virtually disappeared from a host of public institutions, as has a purposeful effort to develop the student's ability to think—sad facts that in themselves help account for the anti-intellectualism plaguing civilization today.

The schools of the church are needed as never before to teach their students the ancient rubrics of right and wrong and the significance and power of ethical perspectives. Reference has already been made in part IV of this paper to the responsibility of the church-related college to train the morally and religiously mature young person in the rudiments of good churchmanship, and – in some instances—to prepare that individual for further study toward Christian vocation.

It is crucial for the institutions of higher learning associated with the church to recover *their historical function as the conscience of all higher education, both public and private.* Indeed, the schools of the church, girded once more with religious truth and an awareness of God and priceless human values, may well hold in trust the very hopes of creation as this millennium closes.

While it is demonstrably true that the school needs the ancient message of the church, it must be said with equal emphasis that the church also needs the school. In a day when *good* religion, indeed, is the last, best hope of the human race, no religious initiative can be effective unless it is intellectually respectable and defensible. Jesus, in the twelfth chapter of Mark's gospel, gives as a part of the first commandant the admonition, "You shall love the Lord your God....with all your mind" (Mark 12:30). What a rebuke this is to those shallow, narrow configurations of religious argument that so often have repulsed persons of sensitive intellect who, had the presentations of the Biblical message been more rational, would have hastened to embrace Christianity. The church needs the instruction of its own schools to refine and occasionally correct its thinking and to require it to be intellectually capable of confronting effectively the complicated issues of a secular age. Only so can it hope to impact the twenty-first century for God.

The historic liaison between religion and education as expressed in the partnership of the church and its academic institutions, in the minds of thoughtful

United Methodist clergy and laity, needs reinvigoration more urgently today than do many of the other worthy causes clamoring for our denomination's attention. Implicit in the renaissance of such an intentional and powerful collaboration is the exciting opportunity to capture and convert contemporary human thinking to a new Divine awareness, as well as to assure that the mind of the church is communicating the Good News of God's love with sanity and intelligence. We do well to remember that most if not all of the great reformations of the church have begun in the environment of a university, a reality strongly reinforcing the importance of the academic community's ministry to religion.[4]

The Schools of the Church in an Annual Conference:
General Observations and Specific Suggestions

The basic relationship between The United Methodist Church and its academic institutions is usually defined in an institution's corporate charter and by-laws. In such cases, the General Conference, a geographical Jurisdictional Conference, the General Board of Higher Education and Ministry, the General Board of Global Ministries (in a few instances), or one or more annual conferences may be identified as United Methodism's representative in this linkage with the school. The election or approval of all or some members of a school's board of trustees by one of these representatives may be required. The University Senate, founded in 1892, is an elected body of higher education professionals created by the General Conference to evaluate, review and approve an institution's right to claim affiliation with our church [¶ 1417–1421, the 1996 *Discipline*]. The United Methodist Foundation for Christian Higher Education, incorporated in Tennessee, is a non-profit, charitable organization created to seek funds for our schools and authorized to serve as trustee and administrator of gifts and bequests designated by donors for specific institutions [¶ 1422]. The Council of Presidents of the Black Colleges [¶ 1423] coordinates the relations of these very important institutions to our church. Both the United Methodist Foundation for Christian Higher Education and the Council of Presidents have amenability to the Division of Higher Education of the General Board of Higher Education and Ministry. There is also the National Association of Schools, Colleges and Universities of The United Methodist Church, an informal but active consortium of educational institutions related to our denomination.

The role of bishops in implementing a strong relationship between the church and its schools is indescribably vital. In many cases a bishop, or bishops, may be named to a board of trustees and thus given a direct voice in the governance of an institution. The role of an episcopal trustee is of supreme importance in numerous ways in constructing a positive relationship between the church and an educational institution. Another member of the Council of Bishops offered creative input in suggesting the following functions of bishops who are trustees:

1. Regular attendance at board meetings and faithful participation in committee assignments.
2. Involvement in the process of selecting a president, especially in the expression of concern about style of leadership, his or her relation to The United Methodist Church and understanding of its positions and polity, and the character and Christian commitment of the person to be chosen.
3. Involvement in the selection of trustees.
4. Intentional leadership in interpreting to an annual conference the theological importance of its mission in Christian higher education, with particular reference to those church-related schools located within its boundaries.
5. Proper leadership in keeping an annual conference aware of its responsibility to provide appropriate financial support for those schools of the church related to it. This is no small obligation, and one inadequately met in some places during recent years. United Methodist students in our United Methodist colleges and universities, in the last accountable year, received $117,000,000 in scholarship assistance, while The United Methodist Church through all its channels provided in the same year only $55,000,000 for these same institutions—items that bluntly document the fact that, on balance, our schools may seem to be doing more for the church dollar-wise than the church is doing for them.[5] To be sure, this would not be true if we take into consideration the nearly incalculable support traceable to what one bishop has called "derived contributions"— gifts given because donors know of an institution's relationship to the church.
6. A constant obligation to articulate with tactful but insistent clarity the "faith and values" emphasis in board sessions and on other occasions. The late Dr. Merrimon Cuninggim, in his 1994 book entitled *Uneasy Partners: The College and the Church*, describes the institutions of his own United Methodism as being among those "deficient in taking values seriously."[6]
7. The allotment of a generous amount of the bishop's personal time to be spent with the presidents of those institutions of higher education within his or her annual conference, which can result in a friendship that evokes an interchange of provocative ideas and assures an institutional head of the church's active concern and eagerness to help. This deliberate deed, made extremely difficult by congested episcopal schedules, demands

unusual dedication to the cause of Christian higher education on the part of a bishop, but can produce results far beyond expectation.

8. Familiarity with a school's charter and by-laws, so that the bishop is always equipped to point out the implications of the formal relationship that exists between the church and a particular school.

9. Regular visitation with students on a campus, in order that the bishop may have firsthand knowledge of institutional life. Again, this will require extraordinary effort on the part of a busy bishop.

10. Willingness to teach an occasional class, become a visiting lecturer before campus groups, or serve as a religious life week speaker.

One bishop, a former educational administrator himself, suggested, "We must *claim* our schools. The church must take the initiative in cementing the relationship. It is not that the leaders in academic institutions are disinterested, but in the pressure of administering the school, the church relationship can get short shrift." If this is so, and the bishop's words have the ring of truth in them, then the leadership of the bishop becomes indispensable in helping such to happen.

A Challenge

Is the secularization of the academy to be accepted by the church without substantial protest? Given the long history of our denomination's involvement in building and supporting schools, and the longer basic liaison between religion and education, this does not appear to be either a normal or a defensible position for United Methodism to take. Particularly is this so when one assesses the grim plight of human society in this tragic era of moral and ethical apostasy and the absence of God-awareness.

What then, to ask Dr. Russell Richey's question, will "connect church and college" in the new millennium?[7] Perhaps there is a role that the Council of Bishops, working with the General Board of Higher Education and Ministry, the National Association of Schools, Colleges and Universities of The United Methodist Church, and the University Senate, could assume for United Methodism. If these bodies, each with an accurate understanding of the proper relationship between the church and the academy, could dedicate themselves to *a vigorous and persistent corporate effort to recreate for our time an institutional implementation of Jesus' word to "love God with the mind,"* perhaps this would help assure for the twenty-first century a new focus in our church upon some very important objectives:

1. A re-birth of respect for basic moral and spiritual values.
2. A telling blow against the dangerous and debilitating anti-intellectualism

that has invaded our society.

3. The strengthening of a reasoned faith *within* our church and the broader Christian community.

4. The training and release of dedicated Christian leadership to bring new vision and commitment to our churches and a redemptive leaven to our communities.

5. The fashioning of an intelligent and strong Christian presence in an agnostic culture.

This paper concludes with two urgent suggestions. First, it is proposed that every member of the Council of Bishops dedicate himself or herself to a fresh and vigilant faithfulness to the United Methodist institutions of higher education located in his or her particular Episcopal Area. Second, it is proposed that the Teaching Concerns Committee create a sub-group from its own membership, or make use of its existing sub-committee on higher education, to take the initiative in the development of a *permanent* working relationship with the three organizations listed above for the purpose of deepening and strengthening United Methodism's involvement with its colleges and universities in the twenty-first century.

Endnotes

[1]   A portion of the wording in the foregoing three paragraphs is taken from my book entitled *A Bishop Speaks His Mind,* page 121.

[2]   Russell E. Richey "Methodist Connectionalism and Education," a paper delivered before the NASCUMC Annual Meeting and Seminar for Presidents and Spouses, Young Harris, GA, on July 27, 1998.

[3]   F. Thomas Trotter, "Foreword" to Merrimon Cuninggim's book, *Uneasy Partners: The College and the Church*, p. 12.

[4]   Ibid.

[5]   Ken Yamada, Office of Division of Higher Education, General Board of Higher Education and Ministry.

[6]   Merrimon Cuninggim, *Uneasy Partners: The College and the Church*, p. 174.

[7]   Russell E. Richey, op.cit.

XIII

My Faith Journey

This is an address I gave at Lake Junaluska, North Carolina, in October 1996, one in a long sequence of addresses on the same theme. It constitutes the only time I have ever undertaken to trace in some detail the structure of my religious life and experience.

One of the very important aspects of this subject, stated adequately in the manuscript, has to do with my graduate thesis on Dwight Lyman Moody. In the long process of researching and preparing this thesis, Dr. Paul Moody, the surviving son, allowed me to be privy to a few facts which at that time had not appeared in any biography of his father. The questionnaire that I prepared to assist in the research brought some very unusual responses from living converts of Moody, including Henry Sloane Coffin and Mary Emma Woolley. Dr. Moody thought my paper should be published and his efforts to facilitate this unfortunately were stopped by his death. It has stood on my library shelves these many years and I have decided that the release of new information which is substantive but not exactly critical might, for some people, disturb their image of America's greatest evangelist.

I have only realized fully in recent years how this earlier adventure in study must have affected my philosophy of Christian mission which has always in my professional years plead for an appropriate combination of evangelism and education. My visit to the two schools in Northfield, Massachusetts, founded by Moody convinced me that the evangelist himself, deprived of education beyond the first few grades, developed a similar concern. There is no doubt in my mind that my careful study of Moody in my early years helped greatly to fuel my work as president of The Foundation for Evangelism.

My Faith Journey

My debt of gratitude to Almighty God, to Jesus Christ, and to the wonderful Christian people I have met along my pilgrim way is indescribably great. I have agreed to reconstruct my own faith journey only at the insistent request of the dear friend who invited me to speak this evening, for most of its details are either already set down in books I have written, or fall into the category of being too personal to reveal in a spoken message.

I am not first of all a bishop, or even a minister; I am a sinner saved by grace. How does one pinpoint when it happened? There were preliminary decisions, small epiphanies, but my soul goes back to a Sunday afternoon when I was a teenager and alone in my parents' house in Johnson City, Tennessee. I had been much engaged in thought and prayer for days and weeks, and quite suddenly it all seemed to come together for me. I knelt, accepted Jesus Christ as my Savior and Lord, and gave my whole life over into God's keeping. I arose satisfied, calm, and resolute in the action I had taken. Remembering now the joy of that long ago occasion, I can relate easily to the lyrical language used by the late Nels Ferré in describing his experience of divine grace: "The birds sang a new song that day, and the trees all wore halos... The very air was softer and utterly mysterious. Never can I forget the strangeness and wonder of it all."

While I have always been grateful for the strong memory of that Sunday afternoon event in my life, I know that not all Christians have such a memory. There are some—indeed many—who cannot point to any certain time or place as the occasion when Christ became their Savior and Lord. God deals with his children in many different ways, and no one of us has the right to impose upon another the necessity for an experience similar to his or her own. Conversion in the religious realm, as in nature itself, can come quietly but suddenly; it can come dramatically, even traumatically and suddenly; or it can come slowly, gradually, nearly imperceptibly until at last there is an overwhelming awareness that the event has occurred even though the person to whom it has happened was scarcely aware of the process. But the end result is the same: a person has embraced the Saviorhood of Jesus Christ and knows that the burden of sin has been rolled away, and that all of life is different.

I am debtor to many. First, to my parents, and even to my paternal grandfather. They were sturdy, dedicated people, poor in this world's goods, but controlled by high ideals and an almost unbelievable loyalty to the church. But my indebtedness does not stop with my family. There was a Presbyterian preacher's daughter, a remarkable woman Bible teacher, a brilliant young pastor, and a dear friend who was an automobile mechanic and a recovered alcoholic, all in Johnson City: each of these in her or his own way touched my life and moved it gently but surely nearer to God. In addition, there were church members, Sunday School teachers, persons in public education, ministers from other churches, and famous preachers who passed my way, all of whom the Heavenly Father used to sensitize my mind and heart to His claim and call. Such experiences were not confined to my boyhood or young manhood but became a lifelong process. I have always been conscious, and I still am today, of the way in which God's giants, some unknown and others distinguished, have kept tapping me on the shoulder. A complete roster of such influences would need to include books I have read (usually by authors I never met), addresses and sermons I have listened to, and even faraway events that have impacted my life through the news media. All of my days I have been a learner, and I still am: to me, being alive means this.

My greatest human debt is to my wife. We have known each other since the fifth grade. We lived on the same avenue, went to the same church, and graduated from the same college. I always meant to marry her, but for a long time she was determined it would not happen. When at last it did, a wonderful new life opened up for me. She has been the catalyst for any success I have had. Across all of our ministry in pastorates, on a college campus, and through 32 years in the episcopacy, she has drawn folk, both plain and famous, to herself by her unfailing gifts of friendliness, good humor and infectious charm. People, for the most part, have respected me; but they have loved her. Her instant readiness to receive my parents in our home when the need came, even though she must have known how great her own sacrifice would be, made it possible for me to continue my ministry. I know the depth of her faith in God and Jesus Christ, a faith that has enabled her, often at significant personal cost, to set me free to serve the church. I have always loved Dr. John R. Mott's dedication of one of his books to his wife: "She had the courage to stay at home." So did Mary Ann.

In addition to persons, there were three other significant influences during my formative years. The first of these was the Junior Mission, a ministry of my local church to the poor families in a factory district of our home city during the Great Depression. This helped me understand what Christian servanthood is all about, and gave me a permanent concern for poverty stricken and marginalized persons. The second influence was the interdenominational Youth Council which two of my friends and I organized and led in Johnson City during my senior year in high school and throughout my time at East Tennessee State University. This exposed me to great preachers and Christian leaders from around the world and gave me early in life an ecumenical perspective on Christianity.

The third influence was my graduate study of the life and ministry of Dwight Lyman Moody, the greatest of American evangelists, in which Mr. Moody's surviving son, Dr. Paul D. Moody, minister of the First Presbyterian Church in New York City, guided me. The book-length document resulting from this study has never been published but is largely responsible for the keen interest in Christian evangelism which has always influenced my ministry and has motivated my work these recent years at The Foundation for Evangelism.

I preached my first sermon in my home church one Sunday night when I was fourteen years old, but my determination to be a minister of the gospel did not mature until a number of years later. Indeed, I explored six other vocational possibilities with varying degrees of seriousness, all the while maintaining my activity in the Epworth League and other programs of my church. As I think of the calls that have come to other ministers who are my friends, I must recognize that God's voice summons us in vastly different ways. To some it comes suddenly, sharply, and with unmistakable certainty, often taking the form of a specific experience or event. It did not come to me that way. After my acceptance of Jesus Christ, which was a definite experience in my life, I worked my way gradually into my local church, surrounded on every hand by solicitous Christian friends who offered me love and encouragement. I spent much time praying and reading my Bible and other devotional literature. I went to hear great preachers and attended youth conferences. Gradually I became aware that I *must* preach, and one day (I cannot put my finger on when it was) I was conscious that my entire being was literally saturated with a sense of God's call. There were times of doubt and even a brief period, during my college years, when I came very close to denying my Christian faith, but such experiences were temporary and were finally replaced with a sense of certainty that was to last a lifetime.

My years at Candler School of Theology were happy years. Mary Ann joined me there following our wedding in June 1943, and we served Sardis Methodist Church in Atlanta together while I completed my theological studies. She taught in the public school system of Decatur, Georgia. My first assignment in Holston Conference was as Associate Pastor of the old Broad Street Methodist Church in Kingsport, Tennessee. At the end of that year, we were sent to Wesley Memorial in Chattanooga where our task was to nurture and serve a fledgling congregation that had just been organized. After five happy years we left a church of 550 people and a new sanctuary, to assume the pastorate of First Methodist Church in Morristown, Tennessee, where we spent six wonderful years.

In 1956 I became president of Emory & Henry College, a historic Holston institution located in Emory, Virginia. We spent eight unforgettable years on that beautiful campus. This was perhaps the most delightful chapter in the entire story of our ministry. In 1964, to our very great surprise, I was elected a bishop and we were assigned to the Charlotte Area for twelve exciting years. In 1976 I became bishop of the Nashville Area comprised of the Tennessee and Memphis Annual Conferences. Unexpectedly, in 1980, I was moved to the Florida Annual Conference at the end of one quadrennium, and we completed our 24 years of active episcopal service there. My alleged retirement came in the summer of 1988, and an illness prevented my becoming Visiting Professor of Evangelical Christianity at Emory University, my alma mater. It was then that we became residents of the Lake Junaluska community, and eight months later I went to work on what was to have been a part-time basis at The Foundation for Evangelism. My tenure as president of this foundation is to be terminated three weeks from now, but I have been asked to continue a modest relationship as President Emeritus, working under the guidance of Bishop Ernest Fitzgerald and Mr. Paul R. Ervin, Jr.

At this point in my remarks, I have decided to comment on a number of things that have played roles in my faith journey, and to offer some evaluation from my own viewpoint of the work that God has given me to do across a ministry of 55½ years.

I have always tried to understand and accept the massive change which has been the most visible characteristic of our world during the latter decades of my ministry. I must admit that this has been difficult for me at times. Let me suggest this difficulty in a rather facetious way: I am still struggling to acquire an understanding of modern church music (I can tolerate it but I don't intend to like it). Again, I have a hard time assimilating the revolution in men's dress, particularly the obnoxious habit that causes so many of them to wear their caps in fine restaurants and even sometimes in Stuart Auditorium. I keep trying to restrain the impulse to remove some of these caps! But I must admit that the revolution in manners that has come to America troubles me most, a virtual disappearance of common courtesy, politeness and consideration for other people. I have always felt that those whose lives have been touched by the Lord should strive to be gracious and kind persons. There was a lovely woman in one of my churches who used to say, "God runs a beauty parlor," meaning that the divine touch refines the roughness of our personalities and makes us patient and attractive. I confess that there are other things I don't like, including carrots and liver, but I am attempting to achieve a more Christian level of everyday tolerance because I believe this is a part of spiritual maturity, and a special challenge to those of us who are older.

I have always been enraptured by the beautiful. I love great music, even though I cannot make any music at all. I appreciate fine writing, memorable descriptions, picturesque phrases, vivid word images. I resonate to the power and the charm of strong personalities, and to the drama of moving narratives. I have always hoped, and wish I could believe, that all of this has been reflected in at least a little of my own preaching and writing. I know such things are a manifestation of the truth that is at the heart of creation, and also of the glory of God. Across all of my mature years, I have clung gratefully to that shining sentence from Sir Oliver Lodge, the great British physicist and philosopher: "I cannot believe it is given to a human being to have a thought that is higher than the truth of things."

I have been an inveterate hero worshiper, although I know this is now almost completely out of style. This was behind my 50 years of serious autograph collecting and my penchant for inviting famous speakers and preachers to my pulpit, to Emory & Henry College, and to the annual conferences I served.

I have loved books, perhaps too much. During my college and university days, and later, my faith and ministry were informed significantly by the writings of Karl Barth, Edwin Lewis and James S. Stewart. From my boyhood days, when my father managed to give me an allowance of fifty cents each week, I have bought and devoured good literature, particularly biographies and great sermons (and some detective stories!). My library before retirement consisted of 4,500 volumes, of which I have kept about 1,500 choice titles. I have written four books and edited two others. Across my episcopal years, I have undertaken to sponsor, financially and otherwise, the publication of at least *ten* important books, including major biographies of Bishops G. Bromley Oxnam and Roy H. Short, the autobiography of Bishop Nolan B. Harmon, two books about Dr. Harry Denman and two anthologies about evangelism and theology. Books are my friends and have led me closer to God. Those I have written and those that I have helped to get published are all, as I see it, an important part of my ministry.

Because of the eclectic nature of my background (my childhood friendships with very conservative Christians and my training in a liberal seminary), I have always classified myself as an evangelical liberal, or a liberal evangelical. My theology has remained orthodox, but my application of it often has been progressive and even bold, particularly in the fields of racial justice and women's rights. I have been grateful for the fact that I was able to lead Emory & Henry College into racial integration during my presidency; and later, as bishop of the Charlotte Area, to appoint the first African American District Superintendent in the Southeastern Jurisdiction and the second in the entire church. I always thereafter kept a black minister or ministers in my cabinets, and in Florida I appointed the first woman District Superintendent, the person who now is our new bishop here in Western North Carolina.

The great historic doctrines of Christianity have always been precious to me: the uniqueness of Jesus Christ, the authority of the Bible, the plan of salvation, the gift of the Holy Spirit, prayer, the coming of God's Kingdom and the promise of life everlasting. My trust in my Heavenly Father and my Savior has remained essentially childlike throughout my life and ministry. I sometimes think of Irving Bachellor's great novel Eben Holden, in which he has the hero utter a shining sentence: "When everything else is gone, God and Love and Heaven will still remain." My theology is simple and old-fashioned, but my concern about the way in which a Christian lives and the application of the gospel to the problems of human society is deep and genuine.

My greatest regret as I come to these twilight years as a Christian minister is that I have not been able to accomplish more for Jesus Christ and His Church. As I review my years as a pastor, a college president and a bishop, I find myself most grateful for the privilege of preaching God's word and the joy of writing about my Christian faith. As I have already mentioned, I remain thankful for the chance to do certain pioneer work in the areas of racial justice and women's rights. I have also been thankful for the opportunity to work as a bishop with my Roman Catholic friends and with the total conciliar movement, especially the World Methodist Council. Perhaps the most difficult and important task ever given me by my church was that of chairing the world committee which produced the new Doctrinal Statement that now appears in the Book of Discipline. It was a joy to address this assignment because of my deep desire to help us recover the integrity of the great Christian doctrines in United Methodism.

If I have ever been able to accomplish anything of lasting value through my ministry, it may have been in demonstrating to the church that it is possible to build bridges of understanding between evangelicalism and certain other Christian perspectives. Related to this would be my longstanding effort to combine education and evangelism. While my ministerial life has always been gladly and closely identified with Christian higher education, I am delighted that these last years have afforded me opportunity to be part of The Foundation for Evangelism family. I have always believed the primary duty and responsibility of the church is that of Christian evangelism expressed in the effective communication of the Good News not only to individuals but also to society. I believe that human nature can be changed by God and the tormenting problems of the world addressed and solved. We wrestle not simply for the soul but also for the minds, the emotions and the wills of human beings. Evangelism is the normal expression of Christian experience. To have Christ is to desire to share him with others. But evangelism and education must always go together: evangelism without education is dangerous, and education without evangelism is sterile.

Now these final comments:

1) I have loved every job the church has ever given me. They have all been

different, and I have indicated earlier that Mary Ann and I found a special joy at Emory & Henry, related perhaps to our love of young people and our life-long interest in education. I have always considered myself first of all a pastor, and I have tried to bring a pastor's heart to every task and situation.

2) I have two deep regrets. The first is that I have had to be away from home too much across my ministry. Our son had to do without a resident father when he most needed me, and Mary Ann has had to bear many burdens which should have been shared or should have been borne entirely by me. Second, my life has involved so much travel (I averaged 100,000 miles in the air each of my 24 active years as a bishop) and such heavy administrative duties that I have failed to build into my schedule enough time for serious, focused Bible study. Others with more to do were better disciplined than I, and I confess a failure I should have been able to avoid, and which is a source of much sorrow to me.

3) I have never had any illusions whatsoever about being a bishop. I did not really think it would happen to me and my wife and I had to make a very great emotional adjustment when it did. I am not aware that it has given me a more exalted opinion of myself, for I know too well my own shortcomings. I have immense respect for the office, and wish with all my heart that I could have served it better.

4) As I prepare to celebrate my 78th birthday in less than a week, I must affirm the fact that my Christian faith is stronger now than it has ever been in my life.

My creed is still quite simple:

I believe in an all-powerful, all-knowing personal God who has loved us with an everlasting love.

I believe in a person's responsibility before God for his or her thoughts, words and deeds.

I believe in the salvation of the Cross and in the fact that a human being may know that sin has been forgiven.

I believe in the beauty, purity and power of the Christian life and in the availability of divine strength for the living of it.

I believe that the purposes of God have meaning in history and will eventually triumph.

I believe in a life beyond this life for the children of God, in which human identity and personality will come to glorious fulfillment.

Perhaps Norman Macleod of the Barony of Glasgow, friend of Queen Victoria, summed up most of it in a lovely sentence: "There is a Father in Heaven who loves us, a Brother Savior who died for us, a Spirit to help us to be good, and a Home where we shall all meet at last."

God has been wonderful to Mary Ann and me. Blessed be His Holy Name! Amen.